Using the Brain Science of ADHD

as a Guide for Neuro-affirming Practice

I0023562

An empowering
path to embodied
self-awareness

DR KERRY CHILLEMI

AUSTRALIANACADEMICPRESS

First published 2025 by:
Australian Academic Press Group Pty. Ltd.
The Gap QLD, Australia
www.australianacademicpress.com.au

A catalogue record for this
book is available from the
National Library of Australia
NATIONAL LIBRARY OF AUSTRALIA

Using the Brain Science of ADHD as a Guide for Neuro-affirming Practice

ISBN 978-1-923114-06-7 (paperback)
ISBN 978-1-923114-07-4 (ebook)

Disclaimer
Every effort has been made in preparing this work to provide information based on accepted standards
and practice at the time of publication. The publisher and author, however, make no representations or
warranties with respect to the accuracy or completeness of the contents of this book and specifically
disclaim any implied warranties of merchantability or fitness for a particular purpose. It is sold on the
understanding that the publisher is not engaged in rendering professional services and neither the
publisher nor the author shall be liable for damages arising herefrom. If professional advice or other
expert assistance is required, the services of a competent professional should be sought.

Publisher & Editor: Stephen May
Cover design: Luke Harris, Working Type Studio
Typesetting: Australian Academic Press
Printing: Lightning Source

Contents

Kerry Chillemi is a clinical psychologist with a Professional Doctorate in Clinical Psychology who has experience in the welfare, health, and private practice sectors. Kerry's areas of expertise include anxiety, ADHD, autism spectrum disorder and more. Kerry navigates the world as a neurodivergent person herself, which informs her neuro-affirming and neuro-biological approach to therapy with ADHDers. She developed *The Functional Legacy Mindset* approach to educate people on how different minds function (to embrace their strengths) and the legacy of such minds in terms of the benefits to society. The theory of this approach is grounded by the therapeutic benefits of embracing the authentic self, to promote a sense of purpose, in which clients feel empowered to embrace their unique strengths and abilities to contribute to society in ways that feel authentic and meaningful to them. Kerry's personal journey as a mother of a neurodivergent child includes advocating for a paradigm shift towards research informed inclusive practices, respectfully encouraging empowerment and innovation for the good of all.

Important Terms of Reference

This book uses the term **ADHDer** as established and used by the ADHD community. It also uses *identity-first language* that puts the disorder first (e.g., neurodivergent individual), in contrast to 'person-first' language (e.g., adults with ADHD).

Neurodiversity is a term coined by an Australian sociologist named Judy Singer. The term is a concept that has arisen from brain studies that have shown that people with learning or thinking differences are wired differently. A neurodivergent person refers to an individual whose brain processes information in a way that is not typical of most people.

Neurodivergence is a term that describes different manifestations of neurodivergent thinking.

This book intentionally does not distinguish between different presentations of ADHD (e.g. hyperactive-impulsive, predominantly inattentive, combined), and/or the substantial overlap between Autism and ADHD.

Introducing an Empowering
Path to Embodied Self-Awareness

The unique beauty of the *Attention Deficit Hyperactivity Disorder* (ADHD) mind is that it holds a remarkable energy. A Neurodivergent individual is acutely aware of their differences energetically, physically, emotionally, and mentally, and their acute sensitivity to sensory experiences and stimuli gives them a remarkable view of the world. There are moments in which ADHDers feel confident, productive, and inspired, and hyperfocus presents as a creative flow. Conversely, there is the duality in which ADHDers feel lost, exhausted, insecure, and overwhelmed with paralyses and inaction. One of the greatest difficulties expressed by ADHDers is the expectation of having to repeat your best day.

This book uses brain science to promote embodied self-awareness and a sense of safety and connection to help understand how ADHDers can navigate best their world.

Let's begin a journey of learning with an experiential glimpse of ADHD with the following vignette from my own experience.

One of the greatest gifts of a neurodivergent mind is the ability to experience feelings at a depth that is rarely experienced by the neurotypical mainstream. Something as simple as a hug with someone you love, a deep conversation, or an experience in nature can light up your soul and bring absolute peace and happiness. Pure love and joy in its simplest form. Conversely, the somewhat cruel opposing pattern is to feel completely lost, abandoned, hurt, sad or lonely due to seemingly simple things, such as a perceived critical comment from someone you care about or feeling like you have let someone down. The depth of feelings creates incredible experiences and beautiful connections but also leads to pain and sadness that feel like a part of you is literally pulled out. Rarely can a neurotypical way of thinking relate to the depth of these feelings relative to the experiences that seem apparent. The neurodivergent individual knows the logic and the rational emotion that should be appropriate for the situation, but the depth of the feeling remains. It is both a beautiful and painful place to exist but offers the full spectrum of human emotions and experiences rather than the safety and predictability of the emotional middle ground. Not good, not bad, just different.

Most adult ADHD clients report having spent years navigating the mental health care system with little success due to treatment methods that are not designed to meet the neurocognitive needs of neurodivergent minds. The discipline of psychology is evolving, however, with a move away from the idea that people need to meet neuro-normative expectations in order to succeed in life. The application of a neuro-affirming approach in clinical and counselling practice embraces the many strengths and beauty of neurodivergence and its different manifestations of thinking. When we can come to accept ourselves, we can remove the mask that makes us feel hidden, rejected, and disconnected. If a person is genuinely proud of who they are, it helps them to navigate the world better. A great tragedy is going through life disconnected from our brilliant minds because we see the self as broken.

The ADHD Safe Path

The ADHD Safe Path (See the Figure below) includes powerful concepts that form a roadmap for minimising the impact of roadblocks on ADHD people. The chapters that follow explore aspects of that path to help the reader with a neurobiologically informed understanding of navigating the world with embodied self-awareness, and an associated sense of safety and connection (i.e., to feel regulated and related).

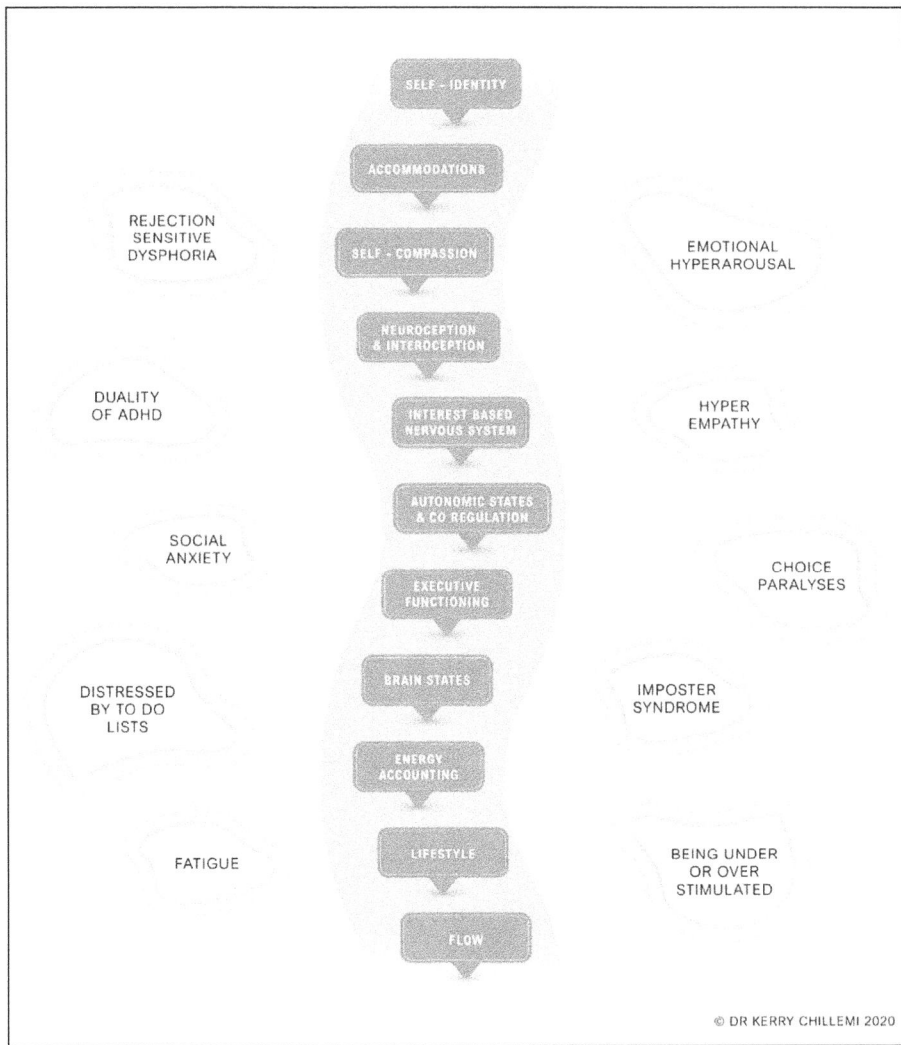

© DR KERRY CHILLEMI 2020

Chapter 1

Mapping Out ADHD Roadblocks

A clinically significant challenge associated with ADHD relates to *executive functions of the brain*, including difficulties with organising, prioritising, and activation of tasks (Brown, 2005). This may include difficulties with getting started on tasks and procrastination. *Time blindness* results in difficulties with setting realistic limitations, figuring out how long a task will take, and prioritising and activating tasks. These concerns result in feeling pressed for time and getting distressed by to-do lists.

Difficulties with regulating alertness, sustaining effort, and processing speed may result in taking an extraordinarily long time to complete certain types of tasks (e.g., life admin tasks) and difficulties with wrapping up the final details of projects once the challenging parts of one's work are achieved (Barkley, 1998; Brown, 2005). There can be motivational challenges in relation to engaging in uninteresting tasks, a tendency to move from one task to another, and achieving below potential due to not finishing what one starts. Research findings indicate that ADHD participants report having an interest-based nervous system, in that they are drawn to tasks that are intrinsically interesting to them and are not motivated by rewards and consequences (i.e., money or status is not a primary motivator) (Dodson, 2021).

Further concerns include chronic difficulties with focusing attention, shifting attention, and sustaining attention. This may be experienced as excessive distractibility and difficulty ignoring the myriad of thoughts, background noises, and perceptions in the surrounding environment (Brown, 2005). Conversely, *hyperfocus* is an intense form of concentration. Employers are initially astounded by the exceptional abilities associated with an ability to hyperfocus (including an ability to problem solve, systemise, and innovate); however, a lack of accommodation (such as not having access to flexibility in working arrangements) will likely lead to employee burnout. The duality of ADHD is described as a de-regulated activity spectrum, ranging between hyperactivity and symptoms of burnout.

Hyperactivity is often experienced as an internal feeling of emotional hyperarousal (i.e., difficulty with modulating emotions), restlessness, and racing thoughts. Social situations can be challenging (as this requires monitoring oneself, one's context, and self-regulating action) and may result in feeling self-conscious and inhibited in social interactions (Brown, 2005).

Two commonly reported symptoms of ADHD that can lead to mental exhaustion include *choice paralysis* and *imposter syndrome*. Choice paralyses often present as running through hundreds of scenarios (for example, what if thoughts about all the possible unknowns). Imposter syndrome (i.e., the idea of being found out or not living up to one's expectations of the self) leads to self-deprecating thoughts, paralyses, and anticipated shame.

Rejection-sensitive dysphoria is extreme emotional pain that may be triggered by a sense of failure or rejection (Dodson, 2021). The reported overwhelming immediacy and intensity of the feelings can cause one to lose perspective (e.g., becoming overly sensitive to criticism or a minor slight). ADHDers often go to great lengths to ensure they do not disappoint people.

William Dodson, a prominent medical expert in the field of ADHD research, estimates that children with ADHD receive 20,000 more *negative messages* by the age of ten, on average. Often, the reality of a neurodivergent child is a calendar full of appointments (i.e., allied health professionals, medical professionals, support plans, multi-disciplinary meetings, group therapy, private lessons, etc.), with studies indicating an increased risk of co-morbidities (e.g., anxiety, depression, substance use etc.).

Common manifestations of symptoms of ADHD as an adult may include problems in sustaining education or employment and clinically significant impacts across multiple areas of functioning (i.e., self-care, maintaining relationships and managing psycho-social stressors such as life-admin/finances).

Chapter 2

Self-Identity in the Form of Integrating a Healthy Sense of Self

In my own professional work, I have often found that in the initial stages of counselling I feel immense compassion for the stories that I am told by ADHDers. Many report a history in which, as neurodivergent individuals, they have endured countless negative messages and institutional trauma (e.g., feeling unsafe, threatened, and/or exposed to chronic levels of distress).

Initially, providing a diagnosis or awareness of ADHD can bring about a massive sense of relief and eagerness to learn. This is often followed by an important stage of grieving for the struggles that have been, as described in the vignette below.

> As a child, I felt like a bull at a gate. I was often told to 'think before you do things' and 'reign it in'. People would comment that I was 'too sensitive' and 'overthinking' things. I struggled at school because I often disengaged due to distraction or boredom. I had a plethora of ideas; however, I was not able to get my ideas out of my mind and write them down. I often took longer than the intended time to complete my tasks.

The feedback that I received at school was 'you need to apply yourself and be more organised'. I was constantly striving to get it right and was chronically stressed. Years of achieving below my potential resulted in low self-esteem. I felt like a burden, with no one to turn to.

As an adolescent I found it difficult to maintain friendships. I was hypervigilant to social cues and felt excessively self-conscious. I presented as either being inhibited in social situations or I have no filter and talk incessantly, with no in-between. My approach to socialising was either a people pleasing approach or isolating myself, by cutting contact. Impulsivity and my difficulty with social skills often resulted in me being more likely to take risks.

As an adult I would hyperfocus on my work, to the point of exhaustion, which would eventuate in burn out. At the end of each working day, I would collapse on my couch at night and eat sugar and carbs instead of making myself dinner. I had no energy left to enjoy my personal life. Activities that I previously enjoyed, such as cooking and socialising, began to feel like a chore, as I didn't have the baseline energy needed to enjoy them.

My mind is perpetually consumed with distressing to do lists. My mind repeatedly asks, what are the things I need to do today? What are all the unfinished projects I have started and not finished? What are all the things in this lifetime I would like to learn? I constantly feel on the back foot and time poor. I know I am intelligent; however, I feel like an imposter, and I don't feel good enough.

When I look back on each of the phases of my life, I can see the level of overwhelm I was experiencing. I have experienced clinically significant periods of anxiety, depression, burnout, and mental breakdowns. I want to be at the top of my game; however, I am also mindful of my mental health. I have always felt different.

An important part of the healing process is identifying the vulnerability of the inner child within and the associated psychological defences we may have formed due to unmet psychological needs. *Schema Therapy*, an approach developed by psychologist Jeffrey Young, provides a framework for identifying how we hold memories of painful experiences, distressing emotions, and physical sensations, as depicted in the following vignette.

> As a child, when I became emotional, adults would ask, 'Why are you crying?' I learnt to suppress my feelings and make it appear that all was good. Anger was an emotion that was discouraged, and my attempts to say no to things were shut down. When I was overstimulated or under-resourced, I experienced meltdowns and was punished for having reacted that way. It was not until I reached a point of crisis in childhood that my needs were recognised. I grew up thinking that something was wrong with me and that others were managing life so much better than me. There was a sense of loneliness in not being able to express the things that felt important to me. With an understanding of how my unmet childhood needs were impacting my negative self-beliefs and coping modes, I could start the process of healing.

The following examples are the application of Schema Therapy in the form of identified child modes and coping modes (Young, Klosko, & Weishaar, 2003). Schema modes are the moment-to-moment emotional states and coping responses that we can experience when we are triggered by situations.

- **The lonely child mode**. 'As a child I experienced big emotions. I felt alone in my emotions with no one to turn too'.

- **Rejected child mode.** 'I feared burdening people or being rejected for feeling so deeply'.

- **The angry child mode**. 'I felt a deep sense of injustice, being mis-understood, or dismissed throughout my childhood'.

- **The shamed child mode**. 'I feel worthless and incapacitated by shame'.

- **The detached self-soother**. 'I detach by engaging in activities that either soothe, stimulate, or distract from my emotional experience'.

- **The event-post mortem ruminator**. 'I repeatedly review my behaviour following a social interaction, focusing on evidence that I did not do well or made a poor impression'.

Inner Childhood Wounds

In Schema Therapy, The origin of inner childhood wounds resides in childhood experiences of humiliation, rejection, injustices, hostility and/or unresponsiveness. We can internalise these messages as self-criticism ('I am not good enough'), shame ('what is wrong with me'), and an impending sense of threat ('I don't feel a visceral sense of safety in my body'), as depicted in the following vignette.

> Lauren has spent her childhood being told that she overthinks things and that her feelings are not valid. She was repetitively told that she is sensitive, loud, messy, chaotic and impulsive. Lauren had internalised these messages as being too much. The internalised criticism had disrupted Lauren's connection to her intuition, and she no longer trusted how she thought or felt. This had eventuated in a perpetual state of people pleasing at the expense of herself, low self-esteem and unhealthy coping modes (i.e., substance abuse, avoidance, self-harm, and negative self-talk).

Lauren's newfound awareness of ADHD and warning signs of distress has helped her to integrate a healthy sense of self.

> I am proud of how I have navigated the mental health care system and persisted in finding answers. With a newfound awareness of my ADHD mind, I am offering myself a safe space to feel heard and held. I am learning to find the balance between connecting with others whilst also checking in with what feels authentic to me. This has allowed me to feel a more genuine connection with myself and others. I am learning to put boundaries in place. I have connections in which I feel nurtured and prioritised. I see a vast improvement in knowing what my limits are, and I no longer feel guilty about meeting my needs. I feel self-compassionate when I am triggered and allow myself accommodations. I feel more at peace and curious about my place in

the world. I am rediscovering my creativity. I am finding flow in working within my own space and time. I feel more in tune with my mind.

It is important to highlight that conscious thought (i.e., cognitions — neocortex) and taking action (i.e., experiences produce emotions — the limbic system is involved in the formation of memories related to emotions, motivation and learning) do not always produce change. For example, when faced with stressful situations, whether triggered by external factors (e.g., a perceived deadline) or internal factors (e.g., a fear of failure triggering shamed-based memories), our body responds (e.g., a fight or flight response). No matter how much willpower you have applied, subconscious programming can inhibit change (e.g., a subconscious urge can lead you to avoid a situation). The subconscious mind contains stored information from past experiences, especially experiences from our early childhood, shaping the way we think and act. Change can require you to memorise a feeling and move what you have learnt (i.e., healthier habits) from the conscious mind to the subconscious, as we will continue to explore in the coming chapters.

Chapter 3

Inducing a
Self-Compassionate Mindset

As conceptualised in Buddhist philosophy, Neff (2003a) defined the three components of self-compassion as *self-kindness*, *common humanity*, and *mindfulness*. The concept of self-compassion is an important Buddhist concept that has existed in Eastern philosophy for centuries. The definition of self-compassion is related to the more general definition of compassion, which is rooted in the desire to alleviate suffering and involves pro-social behaviours and caring and kindness towards others. In Western psychology, the concept of compassion is generally conceptualised in terms of compassion for others, but it is believed in Buddhist philosophy that it is essential to feel compassion for oneself as you would do for others. This chapter reports Neff's research findings on the beneficial effects of treating the self kindly in times of distress, focusing on the interconnected aspects of experience, and having the ability to have perspective on negative emotions.

The first component of having a self-compassionate stance requires that one is kind and understanding towards oneself when failure, inadequacy, or misfortune is experienced. The ability to view the self with kindness even in the face of failure or hardship is argued to provide the safety needed to see the self clearly without fear of self-condemnation and, therefore, avoiding the need to suppress feelings and also providing a supportive outlook for growth and change. Truly having compassion for oneself is defined as desiring health and wellbeing for oneself, which involves gently encouraging change where needed and rectifying harmful or unproductive patterns of behaviours. Whilst researching the concept of self-compassion, Neff found that most people tend to say that they are less nurturing and harsher towards themselves than they are with other people. A central component of self-compassion is taking a compassionate stance towards one's own suffering, and thus self-compassionate individuals, by contrast, tend to say that they are as equally kind to themselves as they are to others. For example, we express concern about changing a friend's way of thinking to make them feel better about themselves, and yet we do not always do this with ourselves when we need it most.

Jill's vignette below demonstrates the application of treating the self kindly.

> Jill had offered to make a cake to celebrate her friend's birthday. Her ADHD superpowers took hold, and she hyper-focused on cakes all week, learning how to make the most interesting cake that she could find. The outcome was a spectacular ten-layered cake. When presenting the cake, nine out of ten guests were amazed by her creative abilities, whilst another guest walked out of the room. Jill's experience of noticing a guest leaving the room, in combination with feeling exhausted, had triggered a tsunami of self-critical thoughts. Jill thought to herself, 'Why would anyone make a ten-layer cake? You are too much'. Jill was able to apply self-compassion at this moment by explaining to the birthday guest that she had a lovely time making the cake; however, she was feeling overstimulated and needed a sensory break. As Jill relaxed in the sun, mindfully eating a piece of her cake, the thoughts dissipated, allowing her to experience the sheer delight of the delicious cake she had created.

The second component of self-compassion, defined as 'common humanity', proposes that 'healthy and constructive self-attitudes stem in part from de-emphasising the separate self, rather than merely building up and solidifying one's separate and unique identity' (Neff, 2003a, p. 96). The common humanity component of self-compassion is proposed to allow for the recognition of the related experiences of the self and other, in which pain and imperfection are acknowledged as an inevitable part of the human experience, as opposed to isolated occurrences that only happen to one alone. By focusing on the interconnected aspects of experience, an individual who is high in self-compassion acknowledges that all human beings fail and experience pain. Thus, self-compassion is conceptualised as different from self-pity, in which individuals typically feel highly disconnected from others. A focus on feelings of care and non-judgmental understanding that connects the self to others, as opposed to isolated self-evaluations, is reported to enable an ability to have perspective on negative emotions rather than suppressing or becoming overwhelmed by them (Neff, 2005).

Greg's vignette below of applying the concept of 'common humanity', explains how he progressed from a state of exhausting all of his resources for coping, to advocating for accommodations.

> Prior to receiving a formal diagnosis of ADHD, Greg explained that his work history was one of a perpetual cycle of ADHD burnout. Greg advised that when he initially starts at a workplace, people are often astounded by his ability to problem solve, mentor, systemise and innovate. Greg advised that it is not long before people come rushing to him for answers to their unsolved problems. Whilst Greg is busy putting out spot fires and saying yes to an ever-growing list of tasks, the insurmountable workload snowballs into one he cannot keep on top of. In the past, Greg would quit his job due to burnout. Greg has learnt to apply the concept of common humanity by seeking support. The employer accommodated this by adding uninterrupted work time, blocking time to avoid over-scheduling, minimising marginal functions to allow focus on essential job duties, and offering sufficient progression opportunities. This was a win-win for Greg and his employer.

The third component of self-compassion, defined as 'mindfulness', requires taking a balanced approach to our negative emotions so that feelings are neither suppressed nor exaggerated. Mindfulness requires a willingness to observe one's negative thoughts and feelings in a non-judgmental, receptive mind state of openness and clarity without trying to suppress or deny them. Neff argues that we cannot ignore our pain and feel compassion for it at the same time. The skill of mindfulness requires people to examine feelings without suppressing or becoming completely overwhelmed by them, thus avoiding the disabling process of over-identifying with their emotions.

Aleisha's vignette demonstrates the application of mindfulness, by redirecting her thinking away from judgement, towards a neutral exploration of embodied self-awareness.

> Aleisha wanted to attend a friend's event; however, she was feeling overwhelmed — 'this feeling is too much, I can't do this'. Aleisha compassionately acknowledged the physical sensation of anxiety in her body without judgment. In order to soothe herself, Aleisha moved outside and sat with her pet rabbit. When Aleisha felt more regulated, she recalled her friend having mentioned that the event was being held in a venue with an outdoor garden. Aleisha made a plan that she would navigate towards people she felt comfortable with (i.e., to experience relational safety) whilst enjoying a mindful seat in nature. Aleisha drove to the event and gave herself permission to leave the event at a time that felt was right for her.

Empirical Studies that Demonstrate the Protective Qualities of Self-Compassion

Although the concept of self-compassion is a relatively recent psychological concept in Western psychology, research suggests that the three components of self-compassion support healthy self-attitudes and facilitate resilience and adaptation (Mayer & Salovey, 1997). The potential benefits of raising self-compassion levels are further supported by numerous studies in which self-compassion has been linked to positive aspects of wellbeing, including social connectedness, emotional intelligence, self-determination, subjective wellbeing, and corresponding decreases in anxiety, depression, rumination, thought suppression, self-criticism, and neurotic perfectionism (Neff, 2003b; Neff et al., 2007a; Leary et al., 2007). Thus, self-compassion is proposed to increase self-kindness to enable negative experiences to be seen without the loss of perspective that stems from excessive self-criticism, feelings of isolation and over-identification with one's experiences.

Neff and colleagues (2007) proposed that self-compassion is a skill that facilitates mental health and is most usefully drawn upon as a buffer or coping strategy in instances of pain, failure, or perceived inadequacy. Having a compassionate, objective, and mindful perspective is argued to enable self-compassionate individuals to cope with challenging circumstances that surpass their levels of self-esteem. Self-esteem is conceptualised as a state of self-acceptance that is based on feelings of self-worth, whilst self-compassion is a conceptually distinctive process that is based on feelings of kindness. Rather than trying to bolster one's self-esteem with positive self-evaluations, self-compassion is a healthy form of accepting one's shortcomings. Whilst it is important not to dismiss the positive benefits of self-esteem, research indicates that self-compassion is an important concept that empirically demonstrates health benefits beyond those found attributable to self-esteem. Having a self-compassionate mindset when dealing with instances of pain or failure may provide its most crucial function when self-esteem fails (Leary et al., 2007; Neff et al., 2007a).

The following vignette demonstrates how having a self-compassionate mindset provides benefits above those attributable to self-esteem.

> Although Jessica was highly regarded in her workplace, she felt like an imposter. It was evident that Jessica excelled at connecting with others and innovating creative solutions, however Jessica felt a sense of dread at the thought of people finding out that she had fallen behind with her admin duties. Jessica applied a self-compassionate mindset, by acknowledging that all people have strengths and weaknesses, and accepted that it was reasonable to ask for an accommodation and automate her admin duties.

In summary, treating the self-kindly and an ability to have perspective on negative emotions, enables negative experiences to be seen without the loss of perspective that stems from excessive self-criticism and feelings of isolation (Neff et al., 2007b; Neff et al., 2005).

Chapter 4

ADHD and The Threat-and-Soothing Cycle of Procrastination

One of the great strengths associated with an ADHD mind is the skilled ability of *divergent thinking*. Divergent thinking is described as an ability to think outside the box and entails the free flow of generating spontaneous ideas and creative solutions to solve problems. Commonly reported character strengths reported by ADHDers are:

- **Creativity**: Thinking of novel and productive ways to conceptualise and do things.

- **Curiosity**: Taking an interest in ongoing experience for its own sake, finding subjects and topics of fascinating, exploring and discovering.

- **Love of Learning**: Mastering new skills, topics and bodies of knowledge, whether on one's own or formally, with a tendency to add systematically to what one knows. (Source: VIA Institute character strengths survey).

ADHDers tend to thrive in situations of variety and rapid change due to being highly skilled learners with exceptional problem-solving abilities. Conversely, there are certain triggers of perceived threat that can lead to *ADHD paralysis* and require a need to soothe before actioning a task.

Commonly reported triggers of threat that can lead to ADHD paralysis (a state of physical, mental, and emotional overwhelm) can include:

- Initial enquiries (i.e., contacting unfamiliar people to request further information).

- Task initiation of administrative tasks (i.e., completing tax returns, invoicing, etc.).

- Responding to messages (i.e., particularly those that require future planning/commitments).

- Imposter syndrome (i.e., feeling like a fraud).

- Choice paralysis (i.e., ambiguity about what the task may involve).

- Rejection-sensitive dysphoria (i.e., the self-judgement of letting someone down).

ADHD paralyses is described in the following vignette:

> Prior to making an enquiry, my mind anticipates every scenario and response that may play out. My anxiety is rooted in the ambiguity of unknowns. It's almost as if I need to know the answer before I ask a question. My rational mind tells me that once I start conversing, the interaction will go well (i.e., I will respond to new information as needed). The memory of past positive interactions does not help with initiating the task. The level of being overwhelmed and paralysed incapacitates my ability to initiate the task.

It is important to be self-compassionate about the level of distress associated with ADHD paralyses.

Decision-making, planning, organising, ordering, and thinking through the consequences of things, is a logistical process that draws from the brain's *executive functioning*. Executive functioning is a complex cognitive process influenced by the prefrontal cortex, amygdala, and the limbic system. ADHDers can experience a disruption to these processes that result in them experiencing difficulties with attention, emotional regulation, and decision-making. This can produce procrastination and difficulty with keeping up with commitments. Conversely, when an activity is particularly interesting, a state of hyperfocus can lead to an inability to stop doing a task and cause one to lose track of time, forget to eat, and ignore other responsibilities, including self-care.

The following vignette describe the level of overwhelm and fatigue associated with actioning a task and a stated timeline of either NOW or NOT NOW.

> I have avoided unpacking boxes in the new house. As I consider storage options and the process of decluttering, I begin to feel overwhelmed by decision making (e.g., what belongings should be re-homed, how will I store my items, what is the right waste removal options etc.). My mind wanders to a meta-analysis of how the house is configured and how things can be best placed. Each task feels equally important to do. My attempt to start has resulted in me moving from box to box without making any progress. Every time I attempt to start this task, I feel overwhelmed by decision making, I go down rabbit holes of researching what is the right way for me to go about doing the task, and I feel paralysed by inaction, and guilty when this pattern repeats. I eventually experience a state of flow and I will not be able to stop actioning the task. When I am in a state of 'NOW', I will hyperfocus on the task and all else in my life will likely be neglected whilst I stay on task.

Karly's vignette below demonstrates how a task of enquiring about cleaning service impacted her emotionally, physically, and financially.

> I decided that I would like to enquire about getting a cleaner to visit my house. When I attempted to message a cleaning organisation, I was plagued by 'what if' thoughts. For example, 'What If they ask me to make a commitment that I cannot keep?'; 'What if my house is not

suitably organised enough for a cleaner?'. My ADHD mind hyper-focused on ambiguity, creating an endless loop of unknowns. My level of distress resulted in me putting down the phone. I began decluttering by moving items from one room to another. This progressed into going down rabbit holes of researching storage systems. I will go to great lengths to be self-sufficient and innovative to solve problems. I become a jack of all trades. Rather than buying a pre-built storage system, I decided I could teach myself the skills needed to build a shelving unit. Whilst I was impressed with my ability to build a shelving unit, my divergent thinking resulted in me not doing any of the things I needed to do that week. I felt exhausted and overwhelmed, and I was no closer to my initial goal of contacting a cleaning service to ask for assistance.

The next section explains how to navigate the emotional regulation system to avoid the threat and soothing of the cycle of procrastination.

Navigating the Emotional Regulation System

Paul Gilbert's evolutionary model proposes that human beings switch between three systems to manage their emotions: the threat, drive, and soothing systems. Each system is associated with different brain regions and different brain chemistry (See Figure 4.1).

During a state of 'threat', our mindset is directed towards seeking protection from perceived danger. The threat system can prime our body with adrenaline and cortisol and contribute to feelings of anxiety, anger, and/or disgust. The soothing system's role is to alleviate stress, to bring about a sense of calm and safeness. The drive system motivates and energises us to pursue, focus, activate and incentivise. The aim is to move freely between the three systems according to our needs.

Important factors to consider is your self-talk and method of down-regulating (e.g., to move out of a stress response) when feeling distressed or overwhelmed. The following vignette demonstrates how Kevin's self-talk and method of soothing eventuated in him feeling stuck between the threat and soothing cycle of procrastination.

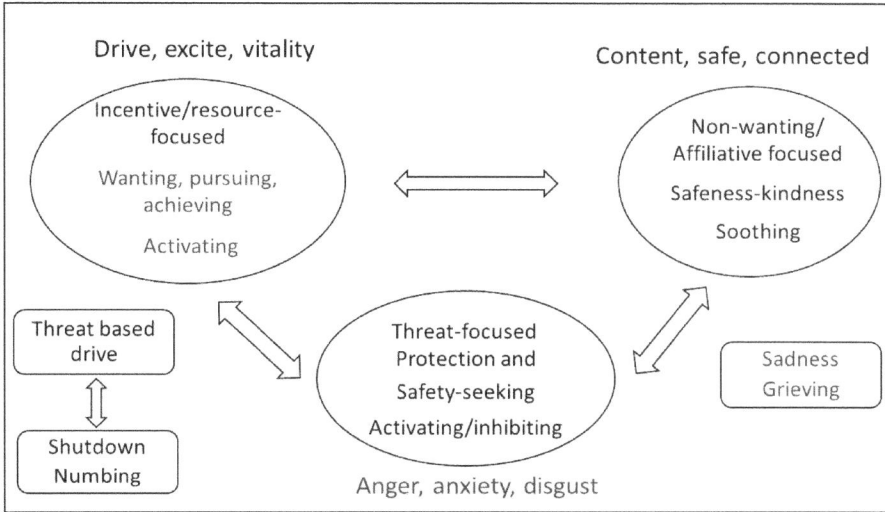

Figure 4.1   The Three Functions of Emotion: From Gilbert, P., & Simos, G. (2022). Compassion focused therapy: Clinical practice and applications, with permission from Routledge. Adapted from Gilbert, P. (2009) The Compassionate Mind, Little Brown. © P. Gilbert

I attempted to start my university assignment, but I began to worry about not being able to get started. As my stress levels began to rise, I felt an urge for sugar and carbs. I self-medicated with food, and I felt disgusted with myself. The overwhelm became unbearable. I began mindlessly scrolling on social media on my phone. As the hours went by, I began to chastise myself in a painful cycle of feeling stuck in self-criticism and shame.

Moving Out of The Stress Response

Once you are aware of these underlying emotional states, you can plan how you will progress from a state of perceived threat to soothing (e.g., a method of down-regulating with self-care) to the drive system (to feel energised and engaged). For example, 'I will walk to the shops to get a light, healthy lunch, and when I return home, I will plan to go directly to the room where my work is set up and get started.' It is helpful to be intentional about how you plan to progress from the threat system to soothing to the drive system (actioning the task).

I know that using my phone as a soothing technique is not effective as I find it difficult to transition away from my phone within a set amount of time, and I don't feel good about myself after using technology. Conversely, walking my dog helps me feel good about myself, and I can more easily transition towards taking action on the task at hand. I also know that it would be helpful if I removed choice from my equation. For example, if I want to go to the gym, my warmup routine will be to get dressed in my gym clothes and leave the house within a short period after waking up to avoid distraction.

Activities that are regulatory, rhythmic, and/or involve movement are beneficial for completing stress cycles (to help the body move out of survival mode thinking). Self-compassion, in the form of mindfulness, can bring about a sense of calm. If your ADHD mind is hyper-focused on an endless loop of unknowns (i.e., what-if scenarios), you can apply mindfulness by observing your thoughts without judgment and redirecting your self-talk. For example, 'How do I problem solve every anticipated scenario?' can be redirected to 'How can I initiate this task without having certainty for what is to come?'.

Allowing for accommodations (e.g., visual prompts, reminders, etc.), may be helpful with task initiation. Artificial intelligence (chat GPT) can be utilised as a template (that can be edited to your liking) for making an enquiry, initiating a task, automating workflow etc. There are several apps that have been designed by ADHDers that seek to create a sense of calm whilst working through to do lists in an engaging manner.

Body doubling (having another person present whilst you initiate a task) is a strategy also used by ADHDers. Two examples of body doubling to initiate the task of cleaning may involve inviting someone into your home or calling someone and starting a task whilst you are speaking on the phone.

Once you are in flow, you can use the momentum from initiating one task to actioning the next task.

Chapter 5

Neuroception and the Autonomic Hierarchy

Polyvagal theory, introduced in 1994 by psychologist Stephen Porges, highlights the role of the autonomic nervous system in regulating our health and behaviour. The theory uses the term *neuroception*, which refers to how our neural circuits detect and evaluate cues of safety, danger or threat. Unlike perception, this system occurs outside of conscious thought. Our lived experience of engaging with the world is impacted by external environmental cues, internal physical sensations, and relational experiences (e.g., an impression of connection, safety, and trust between individuals). Neuroception is our body's unconscious surveillance system that shifts us into one of three autonomic states needed to respond to a situation: rest-and-digest (social and safe), fight-or-flight (mobilisation) or shutdown/collapse (immobilisation).

The Ventral Vagal State is associated with a sense of safety and calm. When we are grounded in our ventral vagal pathway, we are at our greatest capacity for connection. Social connectedness plays a critical role in promoting physical and emotional health; thus, we ultimately want to return to this regulated state of wellbeing and connection (Porges, 2009). The ventral vagal state of safety and homeostasis (i.e., the rest and digest response) is characterised by feeling grounded, mindful, curious and collaborative.

Sympathetic mobilisation activity increases when you are stressed, physically active or if there is a perceived threat. In response to acute stress, the body's sympathetic nervous system is activated. The sympathetic nervous system promotes a fight/flight response. Physical signs of a fight/flight response include rapid heart rate and breathing and muscles becoming tense and primed for action.

The autonomic state of a **Dorsal Vagal Collapse** (the most primitive pathway of response) helps to protect against life threat by immobilising and shutting down. During immobilisation, our metabolism slows down, our heart rate and breathing slow, and blood pressure drops, which presents as fatigue and mental fog (Porges, 2011). Polyvagal theory describes a physiological and psychological understanding of our autonomic nervous system and depicts a pathway for shifting in and out of the different states.

Deb Dana, a clinical social worker who specialises in applying polyvagal theory to complex trauma, advises that it is useful to think of the hierarchical nature of the three autonomic nervous system responses as a ladder (Dana, 2018). We move up and down the ladder by activating the stimulating (sympathetic) or relaxing (parasympathetic) branches of the autonomic nervous system based on the detection of various stimuli (neuroception). The states can only be moved through in a hierarchical sequence (i.e., we cannot skip from dorsal to ventral).

The following vignettes depict an experience of how an ADHDers thinking may present in each autonomic state (See Figure 5.1). This is adapted from Dana's research findings, which show that the stories of connection, protection, and disconnection follow on from the autonomic state.

The Autonomic Hierarchy

If we envisage being at the top of the ladder (in a state of ventral vagal activation), the ventral vagal system is part of your social engagement

Story of Connection. When I am in a ventral vagal state of regulation, I have a baseline of energy to enjoy doing what I love. I rediscover my love of learning and creativity. I have an urge for social engagement. I feel present in the moment. I feel hopeful.

Story of Protection. When I am experiencing a heightened state of anxiety (mobilisation), I feel a sense of urgency, like time is running out. I worry about what needs to be done and feel distressed by my to-do lists. I experience survival mode thinking and an overwhelming sense of responsibility. I am hyper-focused on productivity, often at the expense of my own needs.

Story of Disconnection. When I experience an autonomic state of a dorsal vagal collapse, I compare myself to others. I feel like I have been left behind and don't measure up. I feel like the world is an overwhelming place. I psychologically withdraw and detach. I can't see my way out. I experience hopelessness and existential thinking (e.g., what is the meaning of life, who am I connected to, what is my purpose). I feel fatigued numb, and experience brain fog. I need to sleep more than usual.

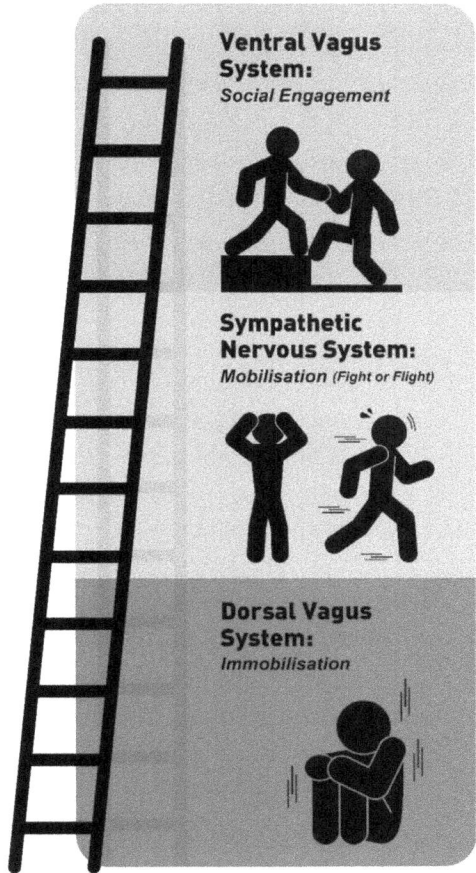

Ventral Vagus System:
Social Engagement

Sympathetic Nervous System:
Mobilisation (Fight or Flight)

Dorsal Vagus System:
Immobilisation

Figure 5.1   A description of ADHDers thinking as they travel up and down the ladder of autonomic response in Polyvagul Theory.

system and leads to feelings of safety and connection. We may move down the ladder into a state of sympathetic mobilisation when the body experiences stress (i.e., as our level of arousal increases) or a perceived threat in the environment. In this state (sympathetic mobilisation), the sympathetic nervous system is activated. If the sympathetic system is too aroused, dorsal vagal activation triggers your body to move into a state of shutdown/immobilisation (in this state, the parasympathetic system is activated) (Dana, 2020). When you experience an autonomic state of a dorsal vagal collapse, it is helpful to remember that you are still on the ladder. If you are immobilised in a state of shutdown (the bottom of the ladder), you must first progress through mobilisation (the middle of the ladder) to return to the safe and social state (the top of the ladder) (Dana, 2020). Polyvagal theory empowers us with a mindful awareness of the autonomic nervous system states and pathways of response. The following vignette is an experience of navigating the autonomic hierarchy (e.g. going up the ladder).

> When I first started counselling, I learnt that I was experiencing an autonomic state of a dorsal vagal collapse. At that point in time, I was failing university, sleeping to cope with my distress, and I was not able to reach out to my course coordinator to ask for help, no matter how hard I tried. My thoughts (it is hopeless, I don't measure up) were not accurate reflections of how I genuinely feel about myself; rather, they were reflective of my underlying autonomic state of a dorsal vagal collapse. I was at the bottom of the ladder.

> I wanted to understand why my body was experiencing a state of shutdown. I realised that the chronic levels of anxiety and stress I had been experiencing throughout the university semester had eventuated in ADHD burnout and then a dorsal vagal collapse. My psychologist educated me that when our bodies experience chronic stress, they can develop various conditions. My burnout stemmed from an overwhelmed nervous system, and the body has a failsafe survival mechanism of a dorsal vagal shutdown. This explained why my body felt immobilised, dissociated, tired, and my brain felt foggy. This understanding also helped me view my body as functional (i.e., the dorsal vagal shutdown was a protective response to help conserve energy) and gave me a clear pathway of what to do next.

> My psychologist explained that I can move up the ladder (i.e., activate out of shutdown and shift towards a mobilised state) by engaging in activities that are regulatory, rhythmic, and/or involve movement. I engaged in yoga, dancing, meditation, breathing exercises, and spending time in nature. I enjoyed the calming presence of being with my dog and reached out to loved ones. Over time, I reached an embodied state of safety and connection (the top of the ladder).

Chapter 6

Promoting a Neuroception of Safety and Connection

To best help neurodivergent individuals navigate our world, we need to create safe spaces. As we have seen in the previous chapter, specific areas of the brain via neuroception, evaluate an impression of safety or trustworthiness by detecting features such as body and facial expressions and environmental triggers (Porges, 2009). In looking through the lens of polyvagal theory, we can understand that although an environment may not appear threatening to some people (e.g., a noisy, busy, brightly lit lecture theatre), the neuroceptive circuits of a neurodivergent individual may trigger a strong stress response.

Neurodivergent individuals are sensitive in different ways to which people might generally be triggered into a sympathetic state (i.e., feeling restless and anxious, increased heart rate etc.). For example, an Autistic person may be triggered by a sound or unexpected touch. I have an Autistic mind, and I often stim (i.e., hand flapping) and react with great fright if a colleague unexpectedly walks past when I am concentrating. Colleagues have understandably asked me if I have experienced trauma, as from a behavioural perspective, my startled response appears that I am frightened by their presence. I explain that my response was not a trauma response; rather, I am extremely hypersensitive to sound, and when I am hyper-focusing on my work, an unexpected noise can trigger a sympathetic state of mobilisation. My partner is very kind, and if he knows I am working intently, he will quietly enter the room with an announcement, 'I am now entering the room' (which I much appreciate)!

It is commonly reported in the literature that a neurodivergent individual can present with 'faulty' neuroception if the trigger is not considered a normal response (e.g., my doorbell tends to make me jump from my chair with fright). I prefer to use the word 'sensitive' to acknowledge that people are sensitive in different ways. For example, a neurodivergent hospital employee (e.g., an ADHDer employed in the Emergency department) who has the ability to stay regulated during a crisis will be better able to perform as a first responder. Conversely, that same person may struggle to sit still in a meeting that is not intrinsically interesting. Neurodivergent individuals are likely to be acutely aware of their differences energetically, physically, emotionally, and mentally, and their acute sensitivity to sensory experiences and stimuli gives they a remarkable view of the world.

Neurodivergent people are however susceptible to *emotional contagion* (the tendency to absorb, catch, or be influenced by other people's feelings) and can distinguish subtle cues that others would not. Professor Tony Attwood described this as a sixth sense and likened the experience to the analogy of a negative tone of voice infecting a neurotypical person at the strength of a cold. In contrast, a neurodivergent individual is infected at the strength of the flu. This can be an overwhelming experience that can lead to a hypervigilant, alarmed state.

Co-regulation and Accommodation

When the autonomic nervous system has moved into a dysregulated dorsal vagal state (shutdown, numbing, disconnection, or dissociation) or sympathetic mobilisation (mobilisation of fight or flight, survival mode thinking), a quest for safety can be realised by *co-regulation* (Dana, 2020).

Co-regulation is defined as how one person's autonomic nervous system interacts with another person's autonomic nervous system to facilitate connection and safety. This involves recognising a shift in one's autonomic state, which is met with a responsive, warm, calming presence and tone of voice. In order to facilitate co-regulation, you need to honour the person's experience (i.e. you are not trying to resolve or escape from the emotion, instead you are emotionally attuned to meeting them where they are at).

Shifting ADHDers out of a disorganised fearful state via co-regulation involves taking the time to consider their feelings and accommodating them by providing cues of relational safety. Co-regulation is dependent upon how the person is seen, heard, held and the ways they are offered safety and connection (Dana, 2020). Co-regulation and accommodation are essential in promoting a neuroception of safety (Porges, 2009).

Environmental Factors

Environmental factors play a significant role in determining our ability to regulate our nervous system. For neurodivergent people, this is especially important. Whilst it is beneficial for an individual to implement a healthy lifestyle (exercising regularly, eating healthy, achieving good quality sleep, establishing healthy connections, etc.), an unhealthy environment can perpetuate a cycle of living in survival mode, leading to the body becoming under-resourced. For example, when a workplace is too far out of sync with a neurodivergent individual's needs (i.e., a lack of accommodation), life becomes about holding it together, with little to no baseline left to socialise or enjoy being outside of work hours. When the sympathetic nervous system works overtime, our body will become flooded with cortisol and adrenaline. A perpetual state of exhaustion and an inability to self-care or feel pleasure can weigh you down. Over time, chronic levels of stress can lead to more serious problems (e.g., burnout, illness, insomnia, or chronic pain, which an overwhelmed nervous system can exacerbate).

The autonomic nervous system, including the sympathetic and parasympathetic branches, helps maintain balance in the body's responses. The sympathetic nervous system is responsible for the 'fight or flight' response, which prepares the body for action in stressful situations. The parasympathetic nervous system counteracts this response by promoting the 'rest and digest' state. The parasympathetic nervous system is a network of nerves that relaxes your body after periods of stress or danger. It is also responsible for maintaining life-sustaining processes like digestion, heart rate and breathing. When your parasympathetic nervous system is engaged, your physiological system is primed to work at its best. The expression of inflammatory proteins is diminished, the expression of stress hormones (i.e., cortisol) is decreased, and we feel regulated and related (i.e., relaxed, open and present). The parasympathetic nervous system, by promoting relaxation and reducing stress, can indirectly support a stronger immune response.

The Workplace

Considerate employers have a collaborative approach to problem-solving and create environments conducive to a healthy working relationship for all employees. Humans have a psychological need for relatedness. The brain detects and evaluates features such as body and facial expressions and environmental triggers to evaluate an impression of safety or trustworthiness. People can either be co-regulatory (e.g., share a warm, calming presence and invite possibility) or reinforce habitual survival patterns (Dana, 2020). Inclusive workplaces encourage neurodiverse employees to feel safe enough to discuss their neurobiological needs and remain open-minded and curious about how best to support the person.

The following vignette describes my personal experience of accommodating my needs as a psychologist and seeing the opportunities offered by difference.

> I once had a supervisor question me as to how I could possibly cope as a self-identified Autistic psychologist when people would be expecting things of me. My supervisor at that time was aware that I had dropped out of secondary school due to my difficulty with navigating a mainstream schooling system. When my neurobiological needs are respected, I believe that my Autistic traits work to my advantage in my profession as a psychologist. It is true that I struggle

with understanding simplistic explanations of emotions and social norms. However, that leads me to remain curious. Rather than assuming I know the answers, I ensure that I solve problems collaboratively with my clients. My special interest in learning about neuroscience means that I will read extensively to provide my clients with a neurobiologically informed approach to treatment. I am a visual learner, and I ensure that my clients are provided with visual handouts to help consolidate their learning. I automate and delegate tasks (i.e., I am so grateful for my IT team, accountant, and reception staff) that I struggle with. It is also true that I am hypersensitive to sound, and I suffer from the accumulative effects of functioning in noisy, brightly lit spaces. Consequently, my clinic space is set up to provide a sense of calm.

Chapter 7

Tuning Into Neuro-Biological Needs

Psychiatrist Bruce Perry's model of sequential engagement and processing in brain states highlights the need to *regulate and relate* before reaching the reasoning part of our brain. Frustration, anger, and fear can shut down parts of the cortex, adversely impacting the ability to reflect, remember, articulate, and become self-assured (Perry, 2020). Dr Perry provides an example of test anxiety, in which the content is stored; however, in a dysregulated state (e.g., during a test) retrieval of that information is not possible.

Dr Perry advises that in order to re-engage the thinking brain when a person is stressed and operating in survival mode, we need to regulate and calm the stress response. Patterned, repetitive, rhythmic rewarding activity (e.g., walking, dancing, listening to music, repetitive meditative breathing, drumming, yoga etc.) can restore regulatory balance (Perry, 2020). Cues of safety (e.g., a neuroception of relational safety) are also imperative to allow a person to move from a highly aroused anxious state to a calmer state (Porges, 2009).

The following vignette depicts the application of regulating and relating before attempting to reason.

> Georgia recently attended a professional development event that consisted of a large number of people breaking into groups to role-play scenarios. As the level of noise in the room increased, she found it impossible to concentrate. When it was Georgia's turn to role play, she was evidently anxious and could not remember the content or articulate herself. Her peers became frustrated at her inability to participate. Georgia felt dysregulated and disconnected from everyone in the room. Georgia excused herself to go to the bathroom to allow herself to calm her stress response. When she returned to the room, she explained that she was distracted by the sound and needed to move to a quieter room to complete the activity. After moving rooms, it was easier to concentrate due to the reduced level of stimulation. Upon reaching a state of calm and connection, Georgia was able to recall the content and participate in actively role-playing what she had learnt that day.

It is essential to create space to care for our body and ensure it is well-resourced. When we are under-resourced, we are more likely to go into an autopilot mode termed a *survival state*. Symptoms of a survival state are related to increased sympathetic nervous system activity, which triggers our body's response to stress and danger. According to Perry, there are four survival states — *fawn*, *fight*, *flee* and *freeze* that may lead us to react to situations in ways that end up hurting us.

> **Fawn.** A vigilant anticipation to stay ahead of a potential threat. The goal of a fawn response is to please and appease to avoid conflict and rejection. This may present as being overly apologetic, being unable to say no, assuming responsibility for another person's emotional reactions and mood (e.g., if you are okay, then I am okay), and placating others at the expense of the self. This may also present as over-achieving.

> **Fight.** A fight response can manifest in a negative way through verbal attacks, criticism, and defensive responses. When used in

a healthy way, you can set boundaries and advocate for the self and others.

Flight. The goal of a flight response is escaping pain to protect the self. Your response in flight mode may look like distraction and avoidance (e.g., spending more time on your phone playing games or self-medicating).

Freeze. A freeze response may present as not communicating or responding in the hope that the threat will pass. This response may lead to feeling stuck in the form of not making any move and disconnection from others.

The following vignette describes operating in survival mode as a nervous system response.

> When I fawn, I will go to great lengths to avoid disappointment. I am drawn to putting out spot fires and responding to other's needs. Over time, I began feeling ashamed at the snowballing impact of not looking after myself. When my body is under-resourced, my thoughts become intrusive thoughts (e.g., I imagine things going terribly wrong), and I experience symptoms of panic. My inability to fall asleep and pain flares wear me down.
>
> I am learning to redirect out of survival mode by self-investing. This looks like showing up for myself. When my body is well-resourced, I feel more hopeful and have a baseline of energy to enjoy my life.

The neuroscience of brain states is particularly important in clinical practice as clients are often offered cognitive behavioural therapy (i.e., questioning the rationality of a thought) as a first-line treatment approach, which may not be an appropriate intervention when a person is dysregulated and disconnected. Traditional talk-based methods of therapy that are cognitively oriented (i.e., that focus on logic and reasoning) are viewed as a top-down approach to treatment. Perry states, 'Despite the well-documented effects of fear and anxiety on the ability to reason, often programs tend to ignore the need to engage the safety system of the brain and focus instead on recruiting the cognitive capacities of the mind' (Perry & Winfrey, 2021). Polyvagal theory has enabled us to become more conscious of combining top-down approaches (i.e., that promote new ways of thinking, such as Cognitive Behavioral Therapy) with bottom-up methods. A bottom-up approach, also known as somatic or sensory-based therapy, focuses on the body's physical sensations. A bottom-up approach aims to regulate the autonomic nervous system and promote safety by targeting the body's response to stress.

For example, when I am overtired or stressed, my mind likes to come up with intrusive thoughts about what could go wrong (e.g., unlikely feared outcomes). In these circumstances, I already know that my thoughts are irrational; thus trying to challenge my thinking does not tend to ease my mind. What I do find helpful in these moments is to tune into what my body needs to feel a sense of calm. When I am feeling hyperactive, it may be that I need movement to help me down-regulate. When overstimulated, I often need sensory rest or an accommodation such as my noise-cancelling headphones. To switch off, I time-block days out for engaging in creative pursuits. I frequently enjoy seeing live gigs. Music is something that I find to be therapeutic.

The following prompts help to consider how a person's thoughts may be impacted by their environment (sensory input) and how emotions may appear within the body (somatic input):

- Consider the impact of environmental triggers (Am I under or over-stimulated, or stressed, etc.) and if an accommodation is needed.

- Consider relational triggers (People can either co-regulate or reinforce habitual survival patterns).

- Have I gone into autopilot (e.g., subconscious ingrained habits or survival mode states)?

- Neurobiological daily needs. Prioritising health and wellbeing, in the form of self-care is particularly important. A balanced diet, time to pursue leisure activities, including movement in your daily routine, and mindfulness can assist with this.

- Energy accounting (discussed in Chapter 8) is a method of monitoring how biopsychosocial stressors impact our baseline (e.g., Consider the cumulative impact of quality of sleep, level of fatigue, factoring in the effect of hormonal cycles, etc.).

The following vignette demonstrates an application of a bottom-up approach to alleviating symptoms of social anxiety.

> John felt dysregulated and disconnected from people at a work event, and he found engaging in small talk exhausting. John spiralled into a plethora of socially anxious thoughts, such as 'Am I doing or saying the right thing?' or 'Am I being interesting or funny enough?' When John applied a top-down approach (i.e., challenging the rationality of his thoughts with Cognitive Behavioural Therapeutic techniques), it was ineffective in that he became increasingly self-conscious and inhibited in his social interactions. He began to experience symptoms of a tension headache. John induced a self-compassionate mindset by recognising that it was the end of a busy working week, and his social anxiety was likely secondary to his underlying state of fatigue (i.e., his tank was empty). John found it helpful to defuse his thoughts and alternatively apply a body-up approach by engaging in emotional rest by reducing the need to be 'socially on'. Whilst John is usually the life of the party, he prioritised his health and wellbeing by allowing himself to leave the event early.

Increasing DOSE (Dopamine, Serotonin, Oxytocin and Endorphins)

Dopamine is a neurotransmitter that is an essential part of your brain's reward system. It is associated with pleasurable sensations, learning and memory. Natural ways to increase dopamine include regular exercise, starting the day with eating healthy food high in protein rather than consuming sugar and carbs, and engaging in enjoyable activities. Listening to music has been shown to increase brain activity in areas rich in dopamine receptors (Koelsch, 2014). Serotonin, like dopamine, is a neurotransmitter that helps regulate sleep, digestion, and mood. It also regulates memory and learning (e.g., enabling us to focus better to retain information). Studies have shown that spending time outdoors can increase the production of serotonin (Sansone, 2013). Chronic levels of stress can negatively impact your brain's production of serotonin. Techniques to manage stress may include deep breathing, progressive muscle relaxation, meditation, and journaling. Oxytocin can have a positive impact on social engagement (relaxation, trust, intimacy, and empathy). When we spend quality time or collaborate with people, we feel good. Bonding over an experience such as cooking can help to promote oxytocin levels. Physical affection or massage can also boost oxytocin production (Uvnas-Moberg et al., 2014). Co-regulating with an animal (e.g., patting your dog) is another excellent way to increase oxytocin levels (Petersson et al., 2017). Endorphins regulate emotional responses (i.e., enabling us to cope more effectively with stress and anxiety) and act as your body's natural pain reliever (i.e., endorphins interact with pain receptors in your brain, essentially reducing your perception of pain) (Sprouse et al., 2010). Research has shown a link between physical activity and endorphin release. Laughter can also trigger endorphin release (Yim, 2016).

Creating a DOSE culture at work for neurodivergent people can be achieved by attending to certain aspects of the working day. A neuro-affirming approach that naturally values diverse thinking skills and provides sufficient opportunities for progression is a welcoming environment that allows a neurodivergent employee to stand with pride and to feel safe to ask for the accommodations that they need. Collaboration among workers is likely to improve communication, empathy, and problem-solving. Through listening to and learning from one another, we can establish trust and meaningful connections.

Ultimately though, supporting individuals to tailor their own support needs encourages self-care, as depicted in the following vignette:

> With a newfound sense of embodied self-awareness, I am much more conscious of things that make me uncomfortable and what I can do to make life a little bit easier. For example, I surround myself with people who correct me towards healthy behaviours (e.g., permission to self-care) rather than self-sabotaging by ignoring my own needs for the sake of fitting in. I have found a tribe of people who appreciate me. Equally, my friends feel comfortable to tell me what they need. For

example, a friend of mine messaged me to see if I would like to go out for dinner with her; however, she prefaced it with an ADHD hashtag that she may need to cancel at the last minute if she wasn't feeling up to going out later that day. Accordingly, we planned to meet at my workplace, and that way, if she cancelled at the last minute, it was no problem.

An understanding and acceptance of my difficulties has been transformative. I sometimes use humour as a way of coping with the quirky things I do to function in life. For example, I compassionately acknowledge in a witty way my need to set multiple alarms, tie things down such as my keys and wallet to ensure I can't lose them and have flashing lights to remember to drink water. I accept that there are days when I will completely go off track or struggle. My goal is to check in with what I need, which helps me shift in and out of states more easily and ultimately feel more comfortable.

Chapter 8

Breaking Habitual Avoidance

In clinical practice, it is common for ADHD clients to present initially with a strong feeling of being out of control. They feel at the mercy of their thoughts and emotions. When this becomes overwhelming, they may rely on unhealthy coping behaviours such as avoidance, blocking emotions and masking distress, which can lead to burnout, disconnection and isolation.

Therapy needs to work toward helping the client drop their mask and move toward embracing their authentic self by establishing a healthy self-concept to foster genuine connections with themselves and others.

Dealing With Avoidance Behaviour

Struggling with personal pain is like trying to get out of a Chinese finger trap. In the first session of treatment, I educate clients that it is our stories about distress and attempts to escape from it that can amplify pain and leave us feeling stuck. The Chinese finger trap (a woven bamboo tube) is a tool I use to demonstrate that when you try to escape being in the finger trap by pulling away, it constricts, trapping your fingers. Pushing your fingers into the Chinese finger trap, rather than pulling away from the discomfort of feeling trapped, creates space, and you can set your fingers free. Clients can visualise that when we lean into discomfort and make room for it in an open and curious manner (as opposed to a sole focus on trying to escape), we make room for healthier ways of relating to distress.

When you move in a direction you care about (e.g. initiating a new relationship or starting a new course of study), new fears and emotions arise. *Cognitive fusion* is when we get entangled with our thoughts and feel pushed around by them. If you are focused on the view of the past, it will not allow you to see how best to move forward. For example, a past failure may lead you to avoid any further study due to an anticipated fear of failure. Predictions can lead to obsessive thinking about feared outcomes and reduce motivation to move forward. For example, a fear of being abandoned by a partner may lead to avoiding ever being open to dating again. Experiential avoidance is when life becomes about avoiding internal experiences (thoughts, memories, feelings, etc) even when doing so creates harm in the long run. The problem with avoiding our negative emotions is that you will also avoid your positive emotions. Moving towards our values is when we decide that something we care about is more important than the discomfort, and we continue to invest mindfully in what we choose to pursue.

The following vignette is an example of a growth mindset replacing avoidance behaviour:

> Having been diagnosed with ADHD as an adult, I have many memories of dropping out of courses, either due to something interrupting my flow (e.g., an admin obstacle that did not allow me to request an extension to complete my assignment), feeling paralysed by inaction (e.g., not being able to structure my ideas into an essay in a timely manner), a lack of interest in the subject matter, and/or a teacher that was uninspiring. This led to a narrative that I am incapable of studying. With the help of psychological treatment and connecting with the ADHD community online, I have a newfound awareness of how that pattern is repeated. I have developed strategies that support me, and I have reached out to student support services. I have chosen a field of study that is more aligned with my interests and will

ultimately allow me to lead a neurodivergent-friendly lifestyle (e.g., allow me to operate in a way that feels meaningful and offers flexibility to meet my needs). I have entered a profession that is creative, varied, and plays to my strengths.

The Adverse Impact of ADHD Masking

Blocking your emotions and masking (suppressing your natural way of existing and camouflaging) may lead to burnout, disconnection, and isolation. Whilst it is important to teach people about refraining or holding back to help with impulse control, repression of thoughts has a different energy in which you are afraid to express your emotions or feel the need to suppress your natural way of existing. Refraining is a healthy response rather than a reaction; it is a choice rather than a requirement. It is important that clients feel safe enough to reach out for help before they reach breaking point. Many clients block their emotions and mask (camouflage) due to societal discrimination and a lack of accommodations designed to meet the neurocognitive needs of neurodivergent minds. The adverse impact of masking can result in physical symptoms (e.g. Migraines or flares of chronic conditions), exhaustion (being incapable of leaving the house or self-care), escape ideation (suicidal thoughts, self-harm), and/or stress-induced psychosis. Meltdowns eventuate when the person has exhausted their response strategies, including seeking help. Social fatigue and masking can lead to an inability to function (i.e., a shutdown) and ADHD Burnout.

The following vignette highlights that although you can teach a person to repress their emotions and not react, this ultimately will end up hurting a neurodivergent person.

> Prior to being diagnosed as Autistic and ADHD, Hillary had experienced numerous mental breakdowns and admissions to psychiatric wards. Hillary benefitted from connecting with the ADHD and Autistic community, seeking neuro-affirming treatment, and accommodating in a way that suited her individual neuro-biological needs (e.g., working from home and setting up a sensory-friendly

home). When long-term family friends visited Hillary in her home, they sarcastically commented that her identity as a neurodivergent person was a fad. They recalled having babysat Hillary as a child and commented that she had coped fine with the bright lights in their home. Hillary was devastated to hear such dismissive comments. Hillary advised her guests that it was true that she could survive a day sitting in a brightly lit space. However, Hillary explained that what they were failing to understand is that it was the cumulative impact of a lack of accommodations in her life that resulted in Hillary experiencing Autistic and ADHD burnout and ultimately mental breakdowns. Hillary advocated for her right to body autonomy and a recognition of the difference in how her autonomic nervous system experiences the world. Hillary received an apology from her family friends, who recognised that their comments were uneducated opinions, and lacked compassion. The remarkable improvement in Hillary's mental health and wellbeing was evident and attributable to her newfound acceptance and understanding of how to tailor support to her needs.

It is important to note that the vignette above also illustrates the benefits of connecting with your Tribe. Nothing is more therapeutic than being in the presence of the ADHD community. It can feel understandably overwhelming when life becomes about therapies, routines, and research. The ADHD community can promote acceptance in ways other people may not understand and celebrate personal gains like no other.

Embracing Authenticity

I do not believe authenticity to be a destination that one reaches. Rather, I would describe authenticity as an ability to check in with yourself at any given moment in time to align with what feels true to you. I often use the acronym **AIM**, '*Authentically investing mindfully,*' as a healthy path towards one's valued direction in life. I start with the question, 'Why am I investing in the present moment'? The question of 'why' keeps me focused, motivated, and inspired to push forward through obstacles. It also allows me to look beyond the surface (e.g., this assignment topic does not feel meaningful to me) and connects me to the greater journey (e.g., completing it will allow me to reach the goal of my chosen profession).

The 'why' can propel me from apathy towards possibility.

Embodied self-awareness helps us to pay attention to our whole body-mind subjective experience in the moment. An example from my own professional life illustrates this concept. I noticed my speech seemed pressured, and I was talking fast to a colleague. My first thought was that I was being authentic to my natural way of being, in which I am free to speak at the rate of my fast mind. Yet, when I intentionally checked in with my body, I noticed that I was also feeling quite hyperactive. I took a movement break to help reduce the stress. Upon further self-examination, I realised I had been experiencing reduced interoception awareness as stress had slowly been building. My reduced internal awareness of my emotions meant I did not recognise the need to implement regulation strategies until the distress had reached a higher intensity.

It is helpful to actively build interoceptive awareness and create accommodations that pre-emptively reduce emotional build-up (i.e., implementing opportunities to engage in regulatory activities) and accommodate sensory needs.

Energy Accounting

Originally developed by Maja Toudal, an autistic psychologist, the energy accounting method serves as a technique for managing energy resources. This approach is likened to balancing a chequebook, which involves creating two lists in which activities are assigned an energy cost. A list of things that sap energy (withdrawals) and a list of things that replenish energy (deposits). A numerical value is then assigned to each withdrawal and deposit to give it a weighting (100 = takes a lot of energy). The stated idea is that when withdrawals are made, deposits need to be made to prevent the account running into overdraft. For example, shopping is often enjoyable for typical people; however it can be draining and stressful for ADHDers. Maja likens it to being like a laptop running on batteries. When just two programs are running, the battery remains charged longer, but it dies quickly when the laptop runs ten programs at once.

An example of the types of tasks that may lead to a withdrawal may include (but are not limited to) prolonged stress, not enough downtime, interpersonal difficulties in relationships, sleep deprivation, chronic pain, poor nutrition, illness, sensory or emotional overload, being under-stimulated (e.g., repetitive work that does not allow one to feel a sense of purpose or meaning), life admin tasks that leads to logistical fatigue, ADHD masking, a lack of structure or routine, and/or overcommitting to things etc.

Due to neurological differences (i.e., living in a world that sometimes feels out of sync with your neurobiological needs), there can be a higher cost associated with balancing the many demands and competing needs that come with adult life. The aim is to reduce the accumulative load and create a sense of balance (i.e., ensuring that we are not falling into unhealthy traps of prioritising one thing at the expense of another, such as overachieving at work at the cost of the self).

The following vignette describes how energy accounting can help you find balance.

> I have experienced crashes at various points in my life that involve features of burnout and depression. For example, I realised the accumulative impact of being stuck in an unhealthy pattern of working long hours. When I got home, I would fall into a heap on my couch, skin picking at my hands and mindlessly scrolling on my phone. I was too fatigued to make myself dinner, so I would end up eating junk food and falling asleep on the couch. I am breaking the cycle of pushing through discomfort, as it eventuates in my body becoming under-resourced. I no longer expect to always be functioning at my best at work. The impact of stress loading accumulates, which means that even reducing the load in small ways can add up to more mental space and conserve energy. I am energy accounting by taking inventory of what depletes and replenishes me. Sometimes this might mean choosing to spend energy in an area that will drain me (e.g. attending a creative arts event in a crowded space) because I value it or I am craving that type of stimulation. Whereas other times I may choose to intentionally prioritise my nervous system health. I am continuing to add to a 'menu' of things that are restorative. These include alone time (i.e., not overcommitting to social engagements and blocking out uninterrupted time at my workplace), being in low-sensory spaces, spending time

with my friends, and following specific processes and routines that work for me. Different mental activities, such as reading a book (rather than scrolling on my phone) and engaging in my special interest of sewing, are experiential deposits that allow me to shift gears towards a mode of being versus doing.

Chapter 9

Three Common ADHD Internal Struggles

ADHDers often describe frustration with where their minds sometimes lead them. They may spiral into intense internal struggles from a craving for stimulation that creates conflicting cognitions around unrealistic expectations. The result is a pattern of thinking that leads to guilt and further distress as they try to resolve a drive for more while constantly feeling unsatisfied. These spirals of thinking can be characterised into three separate types: achieving goals, social anxiety, and finding existential meaning in one's life.

The Activation Spiral of Thinking

This spiral creates cognitive dissonance in relation to setting realistic limitations (amazing ideas vs. what is realistically achievable) in contrast with to-do lists that cause distress. Time blindness and difficulties with prioritising and organising may result in chronic stress. When one's sense of value is associated with productivity, survival mode thinking may activate the threat and drive systems.

Learning to be mindful of your emotions in a curious and non-judgmental manner allows you to change how you pay attention to an emotion and sets the framework for managing distress in a healthy way. One way of doing this is to ask yourself, 'Am I *thinking* my emotion or *feeling* my emotion?' Trying to think your way out of an emotion may consist of thoughts racing, running through scenarios in a panicked state, a strong urge to seek reassurance, and/or obsessive thinking about feared outcomes. *Fusing* with a thought is when the person considers the thought to be necessary, dangerous, or saying something about them as a person (i.e., I don't feel good enough).

When the mind is under high levels of distress, there may be an intolerance to uncertainty, perfectionism, excess sense of responsibility and an overestimation of danger. Intrusive thoughts are catastrophic, in which a person may imagine the worst feared possible outcome and feel distressed as if it is happening. The strength of judgement is overused, and obsessive thinking about feared outcomes develops. Recall that your ability to reason and/or feel self-assured is impaired when you are dysregulated. The mind wants to take control and resist this urge. Once a person is flooded with anxiety, it is important to focus on two things — self-care (e.g., reducing the physiological sensation of feeling flooded with emotion) and what will happen next to calm the stress response (e.g., a sensory break).

The Social Anxiety Spiral of Thinking

This spiral leads to masking, reassurance-seeking, and/or overcommitting to things. These behaviours are particularly adverse to mental health. Subjugating (pleasing at the expense of the self) can lead to exhaustion and guilt. Self-esteem fluctuates in relation to whether the person is pleasing or gaining reassurance.

Social anxiety stems from an overwhelming fear of being judged negatively. It may eventuate in a person repeatedly reviewing their behaviour following a social interaction, focusing on evidence that they did not do well or made a poor impression. ADHDers may be susceptible to social anxiety due to executive functioning challenges with emotional regulation, working memory, and self-awareness. Feelings of inadequacy and low self-esteem can contribute to social anxiety that may have stemmed from past experiences of being bullied or rejected as a child.

Two unsettling things that we face in life are people pulling away and our subconscious urges leaving us in a vulnerable, childlike state. Subconscious urges have a distinct sense of urgency to them. For example, we may rationally know that making a mistake as an adult will not lead to ridicule. However our subconscious mind can trigger unprocessed emotions from past experiences of being shamed as a child, which can lead to a fight or flight response (e.g., appeasing and pleasing). A healthy adult perspective (i.e., schema therapy healthy adult mode) can soothe the vulnerable childlike state within. Calming strategies can help to centre the mind and body. Acting authentically (according to your values) and not holding onto things that are not meant for you (e.g. learning not to subjugate due to a fear of abandonment or the need to please) can relieve nervous energy. Embracing the authentic self (e.g., checking in with what you feel and need at any given moment) fosters a genuine connection with the self and others.

The Existential Spiral of Thinking

This spiral is about questioning one's purpose, meaning, and connections in life. Deconstructing this to the point of feeling lost may lead to symptoms of sadness and grief.

Existential thoughts are those that focus on the meaning and purpose of life. They can be positive or negative. When your mind wanders to an existential headspace (e.g., where do I fit in, what is the meaning of my existence) it is difficult to focus on the present moment and challenge unhelpful thinking. Existential thoughts directed on a macro level evaluate the way human beings act towards one another, nature, and/or animals. This may be particularly detrimental to a person's mental health when they believe that they have used up their responses in their coping repertoire and develop maladaptive thinking about their plight. For example, when existential thoughts are directed towards the self in a punitive way, they have nothing encouraging to say, and there is a sense of being overwhelmed. This may be further perpetuated by avoidance behaviours such as disengaging and isolating oneself and/or self-medicating. The values people hold (e.g., fairness, kindness, curiosity) tend to match people's triggers of anger. One of the most substantial factors in fuelling anger and keeping it going is when attitudes and expectations clash with the real world (e.g., I need the world to be fair and just).

Existential thinkers report a distinct difference in which the mind continues to obsessively return to an existential headspace to question the overall meaning of life (beyond the individual self), and they report not being able to find peace without answering this question. Carl Jung once said, 'Depression is like a woman in black. If she shows up, don't shoo her away. Invite her in, offer her a seat, treat her like a guest and listen to what she wants to say'.

In my own clinical practice, I have often treated symptoms of an existential crisis by helping a client to problem-solve how they can find meaning, connection, and creativity in their individual lives. Clients frequently report that their day-to-day functioning (concentration, mood, appetite, sleep etc.) is helped to return to their natural rhythm once this resolution is achieved.

Existential thinkers acknowledge suffering in the world and imagine a better way, and thus, existential thinking can lead to growth. The social advocates of this world play an important role in the future of our society. I have found that ADHDers tend to be well-informed and will go to great lengths to help others. They give their time and resources freely, often at their own expense. They are brave and will frequently be the first responders when people are in need. Existential thinkers tend to value the quality of relationships rather than status and competition. The character strength of transcending provides existential thinkers with meaning, connection, and creativity.

Finding a Way Out — Fostering Joy and Meaning in Life through *Ikigai*

As we can see from the spirals of thought above, while it is important to allow ourselves to think deeply, it is our experiences that bring us joy in life and make us feel a state of flow, alive and fulfilled. *Ikigai* is a Japanese term that blends two words: 'iki' (i.e., to live) and 'gai' (i.e., reason) and translates to *reason to live*. The concept of ikigai is said to have evolved from a traditional belief that physical wellbeing is affected by one's emotional health and sense of purpose in life. It is a concept that encourages people to discover what matters to them and to live a life filled with purpose and joy. To find your ikigai, is to explore what you love, what the world needs, what you are good at, and what you can get paid for. Japanese psychologist Michiko Kumano has said that ikigai is a state of wellbeing that arises from devotion to activities one enjoys while also bringing a sense of fulfilment. This aligns with cognitive behavioural therapeutic approaches that emphasise the pursuit of activities that produce enjoyment and a sense of mastery to alleviate symptoms of depressive disorder.

Keno Mogi, a neuroscientist and author of *Awakening Your Ikigai*, states that ikigai is to involve yourself in a series of actions that result in the secretion of dopamine, which comes from the rich spectrum of experiencing moments of joy in life. Dopamine is a neurotransmitter that mediates pleasure in the brain and is stimulated by stimuli such as taste, smell, sound and the elements of nature. For example, a weekly ritual of mindfully listening to the sound of hitting a golf ball, having an art space set up in your house to be creative, and the smell of freshly baked bread can create ikigai in life by turning actions into pleasurable rewards. Rather than focusing on one domain of life (e.g. working hard and feeling too exhausted to enjoy life or advocating for a cause to the point of depletion), we need a broad range of experiences to enjoy life from a range of sources, both big and small.

Chapter 10

ADHD Fatigue

An ADHD brain is not wired the same way as a non-ADHD brain. Research continues to show specific differences in the ADHD brain's structure, function and chemistry which create significant differences in how ADHDers navigate the world. While a neurotypical brain is wired to intuitively tune out environmental distractors, control impulses and sustain attention, many of the mechanisms required to do those things are dysregulated in ADHD (Wu et al., 2012; Volkow et al., 2010). ADHDers can become overstimulated because of the way their brain filters sensory input (i.e. what your brain pays attention too or filters out). The mental effort required to filter out background noise can be exhausting for ADHDers. Fatigue is a common clinical feature of attention deficit hyperactivity disorder in adulthood.

In one study researchers measured participants responses to a visual stimulus and found that ADHD participants were not filtering visual input to focus solely on the digits as instructed, rather their brains were paying attention to all the visual input presented on the screen (Bubl et al., 2015). More specifically, the researchers reported that ADHD participants had 138% more 'background noise' in the brain (i.e., a patten electroretinogram measured retinal functions in both eyes) compared to the control group. A further study concluded similar finding using magnetic resonance imaging data showing that all regions of the brain associated with sensory processing revealed elevated activity (Tian et al., 2008). These findings indicate that elevated background noise is associated with symptoms of inattention in ADHD and supports the use of interventions that reduce noise and distractions.

Several types of sensory inputs can trigger overstimulation (e.g., tactile sensations, auditory sensitivity, visual stimulation, strong smells, crowded spaces). When an ADHDer experiences sensory overwhelm, physical symptoms can present (e.g. restlessness, fatigue, migraines, sleep concerns etc). Conversely, under-stimulation can occur when a person is not receiving enough stimulation to keep them engaged, and may feel bored, restless, or be drawn to seek out new stimuli. A state of shutdown may result in hours of time passing (e.g., a paralysed state of blankly staring at the wall). Learning about your neurobiological needs helps you to engage with the world in a way that feels safe and connected (e.g., to feel regulated and related). Mindful awareness can create a pressure valve, that allows you to turn the volume down when the world is becoming too noisy (e.g., feeling everything all at once and a need for respite).

Fatigue can also be fuelled by logistical overwhelm (co-ordinating daily activities). The following vignette demonstrates the benefits of streamlining and simplifying a routine to limit choice.

> One of the difficulties associated with divergent thinking and time blindness can be a perpetual pattern of being late. For example, my indecision (e.g., what to pack for lunch, what to wear that day) and tendency to wonder from room to room whilst getting distracted along the way, was problematic. Streamlining the process by limiting choice (i.e., having my clothes in the bathroom readily set out and shoes and bag ready at the door), and limiting myself to only entering one room (i.e., I would get dressed in bathroom and then leave the house) helped me to stay on track. If it detoured from this plan in any way (e.g. I will have a coffee before I leave), my mind would wander, and I would go off track. Although it feels robotic (and I would not expect this of myself to be so monotonous on my days off) this routine, that limits

choice and distraction, has made it so much easier to get myself out of the house on my workdays.

Removing visual clutter and organising living and working space, can help to make things more manageable. One of the goals of decluttering is to set up the environment to reduce distractions. Occupational therapists can support ADHDers by exploring strategies for improving executive function with environmental modifications (e.g. decluttering, utilising visual schedules), and individualised systems (e.g., assistive devices).

Overcommitting to things can lead to a state of exhaustion. ADHDers are prone to overcommitting for several reasons. The information that an ADHD brain is drawn to and the way in which information is processed is significantly different to most people. Hyper empathy is a common characteristic of ADHD that can result in increased awareness of people's underlying needs. ADHDers are drawn to helping others, and shine brightly with their exceptional ability to do so. However, this can often be at the expense of investing in the self. Rejection sensitive dysphoria, in the form of not wanting to disappoint, can also be a factor. The irony is however, that if you set an expectation of going above and beyond, it will inevitably be unsustainable and ultimately lead to a self-fulfilling cycle of disappointment. Learning to say no and set boundaries is often a therapeutic goal when ADHDers seek professional help.

David's vignette describes how helping others can become all consuming.

> I feel like my body is so easily switched into action when I help others. I feel a great sense of pride when I have made a difference. Conversely, I sometimes feel a sense of apathy when it comes to doing something for myself. This pattern of being drawn to helping others can consume me to the point of exhaustion and eventuate in a lack of energy to pursue the things I want for myself.

Another reason for overcommitting is underestimating the time it will take to do things. It is important to consider what priorities could be ignored if you over commit (e.g., self-care, personal goals) and intentionally time block accordingly. A cycle of overcommitting to things and the accumulative impact of overextending can lead to burnout. ADHD burnout is characterised by pervasive exhaustion, loss of function (e.g. diminished capacity to cope with daily life), and reduced tolerance to stimulus (Raymaker et al. 2020).

Setting healthy boundaries can be physical, mental, emotional and/or time based. When we are faced with stressful situations in life, an inability to integrate our *emotional* and *intuitive* processing with our *mental* processing can create chronic stress and tension in the body.

Chapter 11

Balancing Emotional and Intuitive Thought Processing

Our brain is a powerful processor of a wealth of inputs from within and without our bodies. We see, hear, smell, and feel the things around us, as well as remember our past, imagine our future, and respond to messages informing us about the state of our major organs via our nervous system. Complex neural networks within our gut and heart create their own mini nervous systems and exchange regulatory neuronal signals with the brain. Some of this processing occurs subconsciously as our brain constantly monitors and manages a range of basic physiological functions essential for the maintenance of life.

Because our brain does so much of this 'automatic' processing to enable us to function in our world, we have a lot of time for conscious thinking about many things, including what we do next. Our brain gives us the ability to identify patterns, which helps us make sense of the world and use logic and reasoning to make informed decisions. However, even this cognitive processing still makes use of the myriad of sensory signals coming into the brain, thus affecting mood, cognition and behaviour. For example, when we feel a sudden quickened heart rate, it registers in our consciousness that something has changed about our current mental and physical state. Did the heart quicken in response to our cognitions or some physical action? If we then think about which answer it might be, we are further influencing those states and the mental processing about them. We might remember another time when our heart suddenly started beating faster. This memory may trigger positive or negative thoughts, leading to further mental processing. All this thinking can get us into and out of trouble.

If we get stuck in our heads, relying on the cognitive brain alone to interpret our life experiences, we can get caught in a cycle of thinking patterns that prevent us from moving forward. The challenge, then, is to maintain a balanced connection between emotional and intuitive processing so that our bodies can function optimally and we can make informed decisions. This helps not just in better decision-making but also in better mental health and wellbeing.

Emotional processing is all about 'following our heart'. It centres on a feeling of deep emotions and values. We may fail to listen to our heart and pursue things we don't desire or feel wrong about. It is important to check in with what feels true to us (i.e., what we want and value) otherwise we may think of others above ourselves. For example, a feeling of social anxiety may lead us to self-sabotage (e.g., act in a subservient, approval-seeking, or self-deprecating way) just to fit in.

Intuitive processing is all about your 'gut instincts'— a source of self-protection. This is where our past experiences, urges, and strong feelings converge. It can offer insights that normal processing may be unable to comprehend. For example, ignoring our intuition can put us at odds with our sense of safety or identity (i.e., who we truly are). Intentionally tuning in to our instincts often requires quietening the mind (i.e., resisting the urge to continually return to logistical reasoning) and remembering that our feelings will pass. Instinctive reflections of past patterns can help us shift towards healthier choices. For example, when we ignore our intuition, we may not consider intuitive flashes that help guide us to a more purposeful direction (e.g., trusting that we can move towards a valued direction in life).

The following vignette depicts an instinctual urge to self-protect whilst also trusting in one's ability to be open to connection.

> I feel sad and lonely, and I know that I want more social connections in my life. My instincts tell me to self-protect based on past hurt. As a child, I believed that being a good person would lead to others being good in return. That was not the case. I was chronically bullied at school. My relationships were cultivated based on what others wanted, and I lost a sense of who I was. I became adept at reading even the slightest shifts in people's moods and adjusting my behaviour accordingly to avoid attracting blame or shame.
>
> I have shifted that paradigm as an adult. I cannot always be responsible for placating and pleasing others. Logistically, I know that if I am rejected for being myself or setting healthy boundaries, I have learnt to hold the line of authenticity (i.e., do what feels right to me) as it cultivates a true sense of belonging. Happiness is to be accepted for who you are. As the saying goes, in being uniquely you, the wrong people will leave the party, and the right ones will join the dance. I now know that when you are surrounded by healthy people, they will correct you towards healthy behaviours, they will value your time, enjoy seeing you succeed and encourage you to nurture yourself. I am engaging in pursuing my hobbies, and instinctively I feel ready to connect with people via shared interests.

The following vignette depicts acknowledgement of emotional processing in pursuing a chosen career path.

> My parents convinced me with logistical reasoning to study law. However, my heart was never truly in it. Over time the resistance to pursuing something that was not intrinsically interesting to me resulted in low mood. I became unwell when I tried to suppress my feelings and engaged in emotional eating as a form of self-medicating. I connected with a course coordinator who helped me to consider roles that were more aligned with my heart's content. I was able to use my skills to pivot towards mediation training courses, which instinctually felt more aligned with my interests.

The following vignette exemplifies an emphasis on responding to other people's feelings at the expense of oneself.

> People say that I am all heart. I am proud of the person that I am. I am kind and caring, and people generally like me. When I overcommit to doing things for other people at my own expense, I eventually hit a wall of burnout. When I realise I have no energy left to meet my needs, I feel resentment towards people when they do not reciprocate care in the same way.

The following vignette depicts intuitive processing in decision-making.

> When it came time to move out of our share house, my housemate asked me if we could find another place together. My reasoning told me that it was not a good idea as I did not feel we were a good fit, and I did not want to live together again. When it came to having the conversation and saying no, I felt bad for how the decision was going to make that person feel. I tried to convince myself that things could be different, and my body responded with anxiety and stress. My gut was trying to tell me to protect myself and say no. I listened to my instinct and reminded myself that my regard for other people does not equate to always doing what they need. It's about regarding oneself whilst also maintaining compassion for others. I am learning to show up for myself, like I do for other people.

The following vignettes show how mentally processing balanced emotional and intuitive thought processes leads to confident decision-making and better wellbeing.

> I was experiencing imposter syndrome at the thought of starting a new role at my workplace. I feared being found out for not knowing something or making a mistake and people perceiving me as incompetent. The workplace no longer felt like a safe space. I felt anxious and overwhelmed. My mind was stuck in a loop of questioning if I was the right person for the job. When I pivoted away from my conscious thoughts to allow myself space to process my emotions and check in with my gut instincts, I knew deep down that I could trust in my abilities. I may not be all-knowing; however, I am curious and

considered in my approach to learning and excellent at problem-solving.

My logical reasoning allows me to plan for my wellbeing. I have incorporated routines that nourish my body and make me feel energised. My lifestyle includes a mixture of big and little experiences that bring me joy. For example, I have set up a sewing space in my house, I occasionally enjoy frolicking in op shops, and I have looked up creative events that I would like to attend in the coming months. When my fears are holding me back from engaging in things that feel personally meaningful to me (e.g., anticipated fears based on self-doubt), I process my feelings and intentionally consider my gut instincts. I trust my intuition as a source of experience and environmental cues of safety. I show up for myself in a compassionate way that allows me to meet me where I am currently at (i.e., I have learnt to check in with myself rather than pushing through).

When making decisions, it can be helpful to tease apart instincts from thoughts and feelings as a practical task:

Step 1: Intentionally tune into your *instinctual* awareness of what the next step forward is (i.e., the action).

Step 2: *Rationalise* how you will go about putting the plan of action into practice (e.g., think logically about past experiences and utilise facts as well as logistical planning).

Step 3: Then consider how you *feel* about actioning the valued direction. The heart represents feelings, values, desires and personal connections. How do I feel about this, and how will this impact others?

It is important to create space for emotions and negative thoughts in order to process them. Thoughts that stem from strong emotional processing can overwhelm, often present as feeling stuck:

- Avoidance (e.g., procrastination or distraction).

- Ruminating potential adverse outcomes (e.g., catastrophic thoughts).

- Emotional reasoning is a cognitive distortion of jumping to conclusions based on how it makes you feel (e.g., If I feel like an imposter thus, I won't allow myself to learn new things).

- Excessive sense of Responsibility

The following vignette demonstrates how one's values can influence decision-making:

When I am making decisions, my mind will consider the values I hold true. I enjoy helping people navigate difficult situations and adding value. I am good at systemising and finding a better way. I have an ability to see the big picture, which allows me to pre-emptively solve any potential problems that may arise. I want to do right by other people, and I will go to great lengths to consider the possible impacts of my actions. I feel a sense of responsibility regarding the sustainability of our environment. Ultimately, I have a desire to make a positive impact in this world. Whilst I am proud of the person that I am, I experience tension when my environment is too far out of sync with these values. For example, rather than accepting that it is simply not possible for me to be responsible for the actions of others, I will persist in attempting to solve problems that are outside of my control whilst under-resourcing my body and feeling stuck in the process of doing so.

Step 4: A balanced perspective allows you to consider the rational analyses, the emotional resonance (e.g., processing difficult feelings and thoughts that show up), and instinctively move towards our valued direction (e.g., approaching new challenges, desired outcomes, task engagement and/or connection).

The following vignette demonstrates wise thinking and instinctively implementing a plan of action.

Instinctively, I have decided that it is in my best interest to buy a house. My rational mind tells me that I would need to set aside money each week to reach my financial goal of saving for a deposit. When I attempt to do so, I feel like a failure for getting myself into debt. My emotional overwhelm makes me feel like this goal is out of reach for someone like me and that I might as well give in and spend my money. To process a fear of failure, I applied self-compassionate thinking. I reminded myself that I have learnt what triggered my past behaviour of impulsive spending, and I have worked hard to be more in tune with my mind. My gut instinct tells me that the next step forward is to automate direct deposits into a secure account that I cannot access until I am ready to buy a house. My wise thinking and instinctual awareness are allowing me to reach my valued goal.

Exercises to encourage better integration of emotional and intuitive thought processing

Questions to increase a sense of self-awareness.

- What is my logistical reasoning telling me (e.g., rational thinking)?

- Am I feeling caught up in past narratives of self-doubt? If so, it may be helpful to pursue narrative therapy with a psychologist.

- What do I feel?

- Does this feel true to me? Is it aligned with who I am and what I value?

- Is the likelihood or impact of how other people may feel (e.g., disappointment) incapacitating my ability to show up for myself? If so, how can I show up for myself whilst remaining compassionate (e.g., supportively connecting with their emotion rather than trying to please and appease)?

- Have I considered what I need? Have I articulated my needs?

- What are my gut instincts telling me?

- Am I setting healthy boundaries?

- If someone has crossed my boundary, am I ignoring my needs or gut instinct by justifying why they may have treated me that way? If so, does that feel like a healthy perspective? Do I need to re-establish my boundaries?

- Have I prioritised my time and energy to self-invest in doing the things that I like? If not, consider energy accounting (as described in chapter 8 of this book).

- Do I feel incapacitated to make choices based on uncertainty of what will make the other person feel good? If so, please be gentle with yourself and acknowledge that you cannot always be responsible for placating other people's emotions. They will likely speak up if they want to explore other options (e.g., what restaurant we should go to).

Activity

A helpful activity that can allow you to shift between your thoughts, feelings and gut instincts is to sit and journal.

Step 1. Write a few paragraphs of the logistics of what has happened in the past. Where are you currently at with your decision making and what is your logistical reasoning for doing so?

Example: When I attempt to start a project at work, I am overwhelmed with thoughts. My thoughts spiral: 'Am I on top of things?', 'Am I meeting expectations?' 'Do I know enough?', 'Am I competent and adding value?'. In the past, I would rely on detached self-stimulator coping modes such as eating sugar and carbs and scrolling on my phone. Instead, I will think of a self-soothing activity that energises me (e.g., listening to music), and I will create distance from my thoughts (e.g., mindful awareness).

Step 2. Write a summary of how you are feeling. Also, consider how your decision-making is influenced by how others may feel.

Example: I fear looking like an imposter and disappointing people. This sends me back to the drawing board of rethinking thoughts (e.g., I am trying to think my way out of the emotion rather than processing how I am feeling). When I realise that I am bouncing back and forth between my thoughts and feelings, I allow myself to process my feelings and intentionally move towards my gut instincts.

Step 3.   Write a summary of what your gut instincts are telling you. Remember, gut instincts serve to protect you. You will likely need to intentionally move past your thoughts and emotions (i.e., processing the feelings and not continually returning to thoughts of self-doubt or problem-solving the logistics) to reach your instincts. We need to turn down the noise that can distract us from what our intuition knows to be true. Thus, in addition to self-protection, your gut instincts may offer a sense of wisdom and self-belief (e.g., to trust in yourself that you can do this).

Example: My instincts offer me a sense of trust in myself. I recall that I am very good at solving problems and tenaciously achieving despite any difficulties that I encounter. Metaphorically, when there is a storm of problems that need solving at work, I am the one who can dance in the rain.

Chapter 12

Understanding ADHD Burnout Within the Workplace

Stress is a normal part of life. No matter how much we wish or strive for a stress-free day at work, some days will be difficult. That's something we mainly deal with; however, when stress becomes prolonged or greater than our ability to cope, it can cause *burnout*. Burnout is a state of complete mental, physical, and emotional exhaustion leading to decreased cognitive functioning ability and disturbances in our bodies via an overstressed autonomic nervous system.

ADHD burnout can occur when an employee feels out of sync with the work environment. This may result from a lack of accommodations, sensory overload, and/or suppressing ADHD traits. In addition to a neurodivergent individual developing new skills to promote their wellbeing, acceptance and understanding from others are needed to help overcome burnout.

Finding support for burnout within a workplace can sometimes be challenging. Unlike in the case of someone who turns up at work with a broken leg, it isn't apparent how best to support someone suffering from burnout. In writing this chapter, I hope that by understanding the impact of ADHD burnout in the workplace, employers and coworkers can help the ADHD community by promoting neurological diversity.

Characteristics of ADHD that are of great value to a workplace include hyper-focus, compassion, curiosity, innovation, calmness in a crisis, intuition, and creativity. ADHD employees often thrive in situations of rapid change that reward out-of-the-box thinking. These skills are found across a wide range of occupations, including doctor, scientist, engineer, tech expert, comedian, artist, and teacher.

One of the great strengths of being neurodivergent is the skilled ability of *divergent thinking*. The two terms convergent thinking (i.e., one defined solution to a problem) and divergent thinking were coined by psychologist Joy Paul Guilford in 1956. The exceptional divergent thinking skills of ADHD entrepreneurs are a process of generating creative ideas to explore possible solutions and create efficient systems alongside people management skills. Well-known ADHD entrepreneurs include Richard Branson, Bill Gates, and Walt Disney.

While employers are often impressed by divergent thinking abilities, they are equally as perplexed as to why the employee has not completed convergent tasks on time (i.e., admin duties, responding to emails, prioritising, etc.). The term 'twice exceptional' is used to describe gifted learners with the potential for high achievement (engaging the gifted mind at an intellectual level) while also acknowledging disabilities (without accommodation, an employee with ADHD may spend hours completing a task that can take others five minutes to complete).

Successful ADHD-tailored supports in a workplace minimise the negative and leverage the positive. A strength-based approach seeks to acknowledge the talents, interests, and skills upon which the person can build a life of success and joy. If a person is genuinely proud of who they are, it helps them navigate the world better. This way, expectations become more realistic and do not require the person to meet unreasonable standards.

ADHD-tailored supports may include (but are not limited to):

- Provide a quiet workspace that minimises distractions.

- Allow the use of noise cancellation or white noise.

- Work from home if there are no effective accommodations in the office environment/ need for respite.

- Scheduling uninterrupted work time.

- Taking brain breaks as required.

- Minimising marginal functions to allow focus on essential job duties.

- Assistance with prioritisation.

- Assistive technology (timers, apps, calendars, etc.).

- Turning off distractions — including mobile phones.

- Asking a supervisor to set deadlines for tasks.

- Teaming with another person as an accountability partner.

- Recording meetings.

- Visual schedules.

- Avoiding over-scheduling by estimating how long each task or meeting will take (time blocking).

- Valuing diverse thinking skills and offering sufficient progression opportunities for employees.

Promoting Neurological Diversity within the Workplace

Setting up reasonable accommodations for ADHDers in the workplace does not require lowering performance standards or removing essential functions of an individual's job. Instead, it is about positive acceptance and an understanding that accommodating ADHD can contribute to everyone's continued growth and self-awareness. The aim is to find a balance between allowing an employee to continue to work to overcome challenges and allowing space for a sense of acceptance and willingness to accept accommodations where appropriate. Flexible working arrangements that allow for movement breaks to be taken as needed and days to work from home may also be helpful.

It is important that ADHD-tailored supports are developed in collaboration with an employee to meet their individual needs. Be careful not to make assumptions based on limited knowledge about ADHD or to micromanage the employee. There is a common saying, 'If you have met one neurodivergent person, you have met one neurodivergent person'. This means that what will work for one person may not be suitable for another. Neurodivergent presentations vary from person to person and across gender and age. An adult with ADHD can present quite differently from a young male child with ADHD. Thus, it is essential to have a tailored and collaborative approach.

Ultimately, we want to empower neurodivergent individuals to feel comfortable asking for the accommodations and support they need. Neuroinclusive is a term that refers to an environment that embraces and respects differences and supports the needs of neurodivergent people. Common barriers that neurodivergent employees face in a workplace include unconscious biases, a lack of understanding about neurodivergence (i.e., a manager mocking a staff member for using an accommodation), ingrained archetypes of leadership that deny equitable learning and development opportunities, and a failure to acknowledge lived experience as a form of expertise. It is important to ensure neurodivergent perspectives are included in any training resources. Inclusive workplaces that celebrate neurological diversity remain open-minded and curious about how best to support people.

Chapter 13

Navigating Meltdowns in Neurodivergent Children

A DHD is likely familial, with heritability estimates of 60%–90%. To support children with ADHD and their families, parents should have access to the information that they need to make informed decisions about what they feel is in the best interests of their family. The successful collaboration of educators, allied health professionals and the ADHD community (ADHD individuals and their loved ones) has led to a wealth of early interventions that have demonstrated significant therapeutic outcomes for neurodivergent children.

Meltdowns in Children

When demands outweigh a child's ability to cope, meltdowns present as the autonomic state of a dysregulated dorsal vagal state (shutdown, numbing, disconnection, or dissociation) or a sympathetic state (mobilisation of fight or flight, or survival mode thinking). This may have resulted from the combination of a lack of accommodations, sensory and/or emotional overload, insufficient opportunity to feel diverse thinking skills are of value, and/or suppressing neurodivergent traits.

Differences in the structure, chemistry, and networks of the ADHD brain mean they don't filter information or stimulation in the same way (i.e., tuning out information), which often leads to overstimulation, cognitive, emotional, and logistical overwhelm (Plessen et al., (2006); Volkown et al., 2009). A meltdown is more likely to occur if a neurodivergent child has exhausted their strategies for responding and the demands outweigh their ability to cope. A neurodivergent child may experience a meltdown due to sensory overload, burnout and/or due to their inability to understand or cope with a situation.

When raising a neurodivergent child, people sometimes unfairly assume that a parent is being lax in accommodating to their child's neurobiological needs, despite scientific evidence confirming that habituation to sensory sensitives does not occur (i.e., in fact, exposure to sensory sensitivities for extended periods is likely to increase anxiety and cause trauma). You can teach a person to repress their emotions and not react (i.e., they are no longer disrupting anyone); however, you may not see how much you are hurting the person. They may go home and scream for hours, have nightmares, physical symptoms (e.g., migraines or IBS flares), exhaustion (e.g., being incapable of leaving the house and needing to do nothing except sleep), experience escape ideation (suicidal thoughts, self-harm), burnout etc. Please be compassionate and do not deny a child the right to leave a situation if it leads to physical discomfort and/or if they are exhausted. Just being in a classroom with bright lights, noises, transitions, etc., can be exhausting.

When a neurodivergent child has faced a distressing situation that they can not resolve, repeated exposures without intervention may do more harm than good. You must address the symptoms (with a research-informed neuro-affirming approach that respects the family's needs). Wait to find more workable options and provide coping skills (e.g., a social story of what is expected) later. Change is a process that requires preparation (considering developmental and therapeutic gains) and support (accommodations). The child will likely need intervention before they can feel calm and comfortable to engage in an activity that has led them to feel flooded with an emotion in the past. Ultimately, we want to reduce the likelihood of meltdowns by empowering neurodivergent individuals to feel comfortable asking for the accommodations and support they need. To support future generations of neurodivergent children from experiencing the adverse impact of burnout, it is important that we move towards a neuro-affirming and neuro-biologically informed approach that accommodates the level of the child's individual needs.

Navigating Sensory Overload Meltdowns with Emotional Attunement

During a meltdown, while it may appear in the immediate situation that a child is reacting inflexibly to a request, it is likely an accumulation of experiences (e.g., an unexpected transition, numerous situations that the child could not understand because their brain processes things differently, sensory overwhelm, etc.) that eventuated in the child feeling that they have used up all of their coping responses in their repertoire, including seeking help.

Often, the child will be requesting things in the midst of a meltdown. You will likely escalate the meltdown if you continue to reason with or make demands of the child. When explaining this, I use the metaphor of trying to pour water into a cup that is already full. If a neurodivergent child has reached the point of experiencing a meltdown, ignore the task at hand. During a meltdown, the child will be unable to respond appropriately (e.g., reason, reflect, learn) due to a dysregulated brain state.

In the moment, it is crucial to relate to the child with *emotional attunement*. Emotional attunement is the ability to recognise, understand, and engage with the child's emotional state and respond with appropriate language (validate the feeling) and behaviours (share a sense of calm and connection). Emotional dismissal and/or misattunement are crippling for a neurodivergent child who cannot easily bypass contempt and strongly need a deep and authentic connection.

Do not constrain the child (unless they are at risk of harm). Provide a calm environment by reducing sensory stimulation. Limit talking as words are a form of stimulation. If you cannot provide a calm environment (e.g. you cannot create silence in a classroom), navigate the child towards a location or activity that allows them to experience a sensory break, with a continual focus on emotional attunement. This is known as the *GPS Method*. The principle is that a GPS will direct you where to go next: 'Now, turn left at the next intersection.' In such circumstances, navigate the child toward what to do next by giving them a sense of purpose or utilising a grounding technique (e.g. feed the chickens, take an important note to the principal, help return a book to the library, go for a walk to get a cold drink). For example, say to the child, 'Let's take a break and go together to feed the chickens'. The child may try to pull you back into discussing the problem; explicitly state in a calm, compassionate tone, 'I can see you were feeling (angry, sad, etc.). I know it's hard. I am here — let's take a break and go together to feed the chickens. Physical exercise effectively reduces physiological symptoms and removes the child from the situation if needed (e.g., skipping to go do an errand with the child).

Navigating ADHD and/or Autistic Burnout

Burnout is a consequence of chronic stress, causing disturbance to physical (autonomic nervous system) and mental functioning. If a child is experiencing symptoms of ADHD or Autistic burnout, they may appear to regress — becoming less flexible in their thinking and reaching meltdown more easily — and will present with increased reactivity (e.g., behavioural concerns). Please understand that the child's cup is full, and the addition of any further stimuli will likely exacerbate a dysregulated state and likely trigger shame.

While self-care is a particularly important approach for treating symptoms of burnout (a balanced diet, sleeping, creating opportunities for being vs. doing, etc.), what is essential for treating Autistic and ADHD burnout is increasing the level of accommodations to ensure the environment is more in sync with the child's individual needs. Activities that are regulatory, rhythmic, and/or involve movement are beneficial for completing stress cycles (to help the body move out of survival mode thinking). Neurodiverse minds need to rest and recharge. There are many different types of rest, including sensory, creative, emotional, and social rest. Equitable learning recognises that each person has different circumstances and bodily needs whilst actioning the allocation of resources and opportunities needed to reach an equal outcome.

The following vignette demonstrates an educator accommodating in an inclusive manner that celebrates the student's sense of embodied self-awareness.

> Johhny, I noticed that you are tapping your pencil on the desk while listening attentively to my instructions. That is quite a clever technique, as rhythmic activity helps you regulate. It's great that you are instinctively tuning into your natural biological rhythm. As we are in a classroom setting, the noise is distracting some people, so let's go together and choose a fidget toy or get you something to draw on as a less distracting way of accommodating your needs. It is so wonderful to have such curious and excited learners in our class.

Promoting a Neuroception of Safety

Neuroception is a subconscious detection of threat and safety. One way we can support a child in feeling safe at school is to co-regulate. Co-regulation depends on how the child is seen, heard, and offered a neuroception of safety — a reduction of cues of danger and the experience of safety cues via connection (Porges, 2009). Co-regulation is defined as how one person's autonomic nervous system interacts with another person's autonomic nervous system in a way that facilitates connection and safety. This involves recognising a shift in one's autonomic state with a responsive, warm, calming presence and tone of voice. To facilitate co-regulation, you need to honour the person's experience (i.e., you are not trying to resolve or escape from the emotion; rather you are emotionally attuned to meeting them where they are). Demonstrating a desire to understand and an ability to respect the child's inner world is also beneficial for influencing social and emotional development (self-regulation, attachment, and a sense of self).

Embodied self-awareness is also key to navigating the world in a way that feels safe and connected. One way to support this is to create an awareness of strategies the child finds effective to down-regulate and/or concentrate (e.g., drawing to help with concentration, a wobble chair, fidgets, visual prompts, etc.). Create sensory safe spaces (e.g., a sensory pod within the classroom) and practices (e.g., a lunchtime club) that allow children to down-regulate their nervous system. We want to empower neurodivergent children to embrace their authentic selves and to feel comfortable asking for the accommodations that they need.

When a child is not allowed a necessary accommodation, it can put the child at risk of being unsafe (i.e., they are not experiencing a visceral sense of safety in their body), and/or the accumulative effects can impact mental and physical wellbeing. The following vignette describes a neurodivergent child's experience of navigating a mainstream schooling system without accommodation.

> My functioning within a classroom environment tends to fluctuate due to neuro-fatigue. This means that on some days I can perform a task, and on other days, I cannot. I am highly aware of my surroundings and experience sensory overwhelm. I also tend to notice subtle emotional cues that others do not (i.e., I absorb other people's emotions). I have difficulty processing information in class when a lot of information is presented orally. Without an option for accommodating, I become physically and mentally exhausted. When I communicate that I need space to down-regulate (e.g., I ask to observe and draw to calm myself), I am told that we need to stick to the group plan. When the demands outweigh my ability to cope, I experience a meltdown. Sometimes, I am punished for my behaviour during the meltdown. It is harmful to me if I reach a crisis point before my need for a break is accepted. Once I have reached a state of burnout, I have diminished capacity to cope with daily life, sensory input and/or social interaction, and I can no longer go to school at all.

We must ensure that school staff are provided with research-informed evidence to support neurodivergent children who experience meltdowns, burnout, and demand-avoidance behaviours. This will prevent ineffective and sometimes harmful advice (repeated negative exposures or consequences) from being given to families and reduce educator, parental, and student distress.

Chapter 14

Utilising Evidenced-Based Practices with Neurodivergent Children

In her book *Beyond Behaviors*, Paediatric psychologist Dr Mona Delahooke discusses the implementation of a neuroscience research-informed treatment model that is respectful and inclusive. Delahooke's research findings in school settings highlighted a need to move away from viewing a behaviour as the target, as what you can visibly see is just the tip of the iceberg. Underneath the waterline, hidden below, is what has contributed to the behaviour (i.e., what is happening inside the body and brain that is not visible). The paradigm shift is to view a challenging behaviour as a signal to something important (e.g., a child's body-based and emotional needs), with a compassionate and holistic approach that promotes a sense of relational safety.

Delahooke states, 'I no longer work on behaviours. I work on supporting relationships and nervous systems and looking to the underlying sources of challenges'. She explains that a child who is struggling does not necessarily choose to be difficult. Instead, they may be experiencing a stress response. The first question in this instance is not how we get rid of this behaviour but rather what the behaviour tells us about the child's struggle. Dr Dela Hooke talks about the body budget in terms of the accumulative impact of layers of stress loading. For example, the cost of being in the classroom will differ for each student due to differences in how they process sensory information. A neurodivergent child moving their body may indicate that they need a higher level of accommodation, need for relational support (i.e. coregulation) and/or acceptance (Delahooke, 2019). Compassionately checking in with the child is a key part of understanding what lies beyond behaviours.

Psychologist Ross Green's *Collaborative Problem-Solving* model (CPS) is based on the premise that challenging behaviour occurs when the demands and expectations being placed on a child exceed their capacity to respond adaptively (e.g., executive functioning skills, developmental and self-regulation ability, emotional and sensory processing difficulties). The model is an evidence-based and trauma-informed model of care. Doing well is defined differently for each child to ensure that the classroom is an equitable learning environment. Greene states, 'Kids do well if they can'. The CPS model provides a practical framework for understanding the difficulties of children with behavioural challenges (e.g., school refusal may be a behaviour of concern that can be traced back to difficulty with completing an academic task at school) and employs a curious and empathic approach that engages children (i.e., the children have a voice and sense of agency). Children are asked what is getting in their way, and they are proactively involved in solving the problems affecting their lives.

Without the implementation of a CPS approach, unsolved problems will remain unaddressed. For example, if a neurodivergent child struggles to do an essay, applying a behavioural approach (i.e., a model of either a reward or consequence) will be ineffective for a child with an interest-based nervous system and executive functioning concerns. Unsolved problems in this instance may include helping the child to structure their ideas with a visual support for tasks analysis. Checking in with the child may have also revealed that they were disengaging and becoming distressed due to difficulty with processing oral language. A lot of information in the classroom is presented orally, and in this instance, it would be helpful to provide a visual schedule and visual learning strategies.

Greene's book *Lost at School* highlights how the CPS model offers a new conceptual framework for: '(1) understanding the factors that set the stage for challenging behaviour in kids; (2) creating mechanisms for helping these kids that are predominantly proactive instead of reactive; and (3) creating processes so people can work on problems collaboratively'.

A Neuro-Affirming Approach

Many neurodivergent children learn to mask their behaviours to fit in and be accepted due to an unhealthy assumption that neurotypical social skills are the only way to succeed in life. Masking is not only physically and emotionally exhausting, but it is also particularly adverse for mental health (anxiety, depression), self-perception, and self-esteem, and it may trigger burnout. Insights into psychology have included a move away from the expectation to meet neuro-normative standard (due to the clinically significant adverse impact of repression and masking) towards a mindset of celebrating diversity.

A neuro-affirming approach actively values the contribution of diverse thinking skills. Allowing students to actively participate in their learning goals will likely enhance engagement and aid in supporting students with an interest-based nervous system. Flexibility allows for a recognition that people think and learn differently. This may include being open to utilising different programs suggested by allied health professionals to support individualised learning. It is important that the classroom is equitable and allows for accommodation to the level of the child's individual needs.

The following vignette describes a journey towards self-compassion, acceptance and pride.

> Prior to my diagnosis of ADHD, I had maintained a negative self-image of being someone who is not able to achieve or live up to their

potential. At best, I was coasting at school due to being intelligent however I did not feel capable of making things happen. I had trouble keeping track of schoolwork, staying organised, following directions and completing homework. When I was overwhelmed, I would freeze (i.e., shut down) or flee (i.e., not commit to things). This impacted my self-esteem and relationships. When I did not commit to things, people thought I was either lazy, stupid, or did not care. I was also more likely to isolate myself and less likely to try new things. I feel compassion for my younger self as I now know that ADHD brains function differently, and I have a beautiful mind. With a newfound understanding of how to navigate the world in a way that feels in tune with my needs, I have experienced a great sense of pride and connection. I am contributing in a way that feels authentic and meaningful to me.

A School-Based Approach

There is an ever-growing evidence base for allowing students to take ownership of their learning by providing a flexible environment that fosters innovation and a student's ability to make formative decisions based on facts. This is often aided by adaptive learning platforms and modern forms of education technology to enhance the learning experience.

Neurodivergent children have a zest for learning and a unique ability to focus intently on topics they are especially interested in. A childlike curiosity provides meaning, whether with people, objects, or stimuli. Creating an educational environment conducive to an ADHDer's neurobiological needs involves allowing them to feel a visceral sense of safety and connection and that their diverse thinking skills are valued.

Peter Hutton is an Australian educational leader renowned for his transformative insights and dedication to innovative, student-empowered learning. Hutton founded the *Future Schools Alliance* to support schools worldwide and foster collaboration and innovation. Students work in partnership with their teacher to encourage independence and proactively take charge of their learning outcomes. Hutton's approach to student-led learning with neurodivergent children is seen to empower them through fostering autonomy, promoting strengths-based approaches and creating a supportive learning environment.

Chapter 15

A Pathway Towards Wholeness — Jungian Shadow Work

'The meeting with oneself is, at first, the meeting with one's shadow. One must learn to know oneself to know who one is. A man who is possessed by his shadow is always standing in his own light and falling into his own traps... living below his own level'. — Carl Jung.

C arl Jung defined the collective unconscious as the repository of inherited knowledge and experiences shared by a particular culture or society (e.g., social events such as holidays and rituals performed across different cultures and generational belief systems). The personal unconscious is the repository of an individual's personal experiences (e.g., memories, perceptions and beliefs). According to Jung, your *persona* is the social mask you wear and present to the world. The term originates from the Greek word for the masks that ancient actors used, symbolising the roles people play in public. The persona is an adaptation to the external world; through this adaptation, the incompatible parts of oneself create what Jung called the *personal shadow*.

The personal shadow represents a collection of repressed aspects of our identity (e.g., personal attributes, impulses or qualities).

Children have a biological need for safety and connection (i.e., a sense of belonging), and the persona grows out of the need in childhood to adapt to the expectations of others (e.g., expectations of our parents, teachers and peers). As children, we act on impulse and look to avoid sources of pain. When children express certain parts of themselves, they may receive negative environmental cues. For example, a parent reprimanding a child for an outburst of emotion ('you are too sensitive'), or an educator shaming a child for a behaviour ('that form of self-expression is too much'). In Jungian theory, *shadow work* requires one to delve deeply into exploring the unconscious aspects of our identity that we have repressed to correctly assimilate the shadow into conscious self-awareness.

> As a child, I knew I was different from the other children. I felt disorganised when I would forget to bring things to class. I had a wealth of ideas; however, I was not able to sort them into a structured essay in a timely manner. That would lead to panic to hand something in after the due date. I was always behind in my work at school, and when the teacher reminded me that the workload would increase in later years, I felt fear and despair. I felt unreliable as I was always late to things. I had no concept of time. When it was approaching time to leave the house, I still thought I could stop and do 10 things on the way and still make it on time. I was told I was untidy and often got into trouble because my room looked messy. The shadow dynamic manifested in low self-esteem. I experienced shame spirals about the ways in which I had acted in my younger years. As I grew older, I became a people pleaser. My social persona was constantly changing to be everything for everyone. I loved helping others and overcommitted to things at my own expense. I learnt to hide my struggles and make it appear that I was good, and then I would collapse at the end of each day. An ADHD diagnosis helped me to understand how my brain works. Prior to diagnosis, I had thought that there was something wrong with me and that other people were managing things better than me. A journey of healing (i.e., integration of the shadow aspect of the self) was facilitated through self-compassion, connecting with my tribe (ADHDers), and embracing my unique strengths. The transformative power of getting

to know oneself has led to greater freedom of agency and self-expression in my life. I am engaging with the world in a way that feels authentic and meaningful to me.

At the heart of shadow work is developing self-awareness, self-acceptance, and self-compassion, as depicted in the following vignette.

> An ADHD diagnosis has helped me to understand, accept and embrace a healthy sense of self. I have been gifted with a problem-solving mind, and it brings me great joy to do so. I have an interest-based nervous system and tend to flourish in environments that value diverse thinking skills. Hyperempathy has led me to engage with the world on a deep level. I am passionate, witty, and fun. My interests are varied. With this newfound awareness, I am remembering to check in with what feels authentic to me and self-invest mindfully.

The Process of Self-Realisation

Problems can arise when a person overly identifies with their social persona and cannot access the depth of their authentic self (i.e., what feels true to them as an individual). A pathway towards wholeness is assimilating the shadow into who we are. For example, if a parent valued conformity and discouraged any form of self-expression, the process of individuation would be to embrace expression as an important aspect of oneself. Jung saw the process of self-realisation as the discovery of finding oneself, to move towards psychological wholeness. Through the individuation process, we increase our consciousness to achieve harmony and growth.

The following vignette depicts recognising, acknowledging, and integrating different aspects of oneself in a neurodivergent adult.

> As a child, I was rewarded for my academic achievements in science. It was irrelevant where my interests lay, as others dictated my path. I was naturally inclined to be creative however these pursuits were discouraged. As a child, I had no healthy space to express anger. I was encouraged to conform without question. I felt like I had to silence

myself from speaking my truth. There was a strong emphasis on being a member of society who was known to make others happy. My father modelled a selfless persona. I grew to believe that affection from my parents was associated with achieving or pleasing others. I would feel that I would have to give in to what other people want, or they wouldn't accept me. The assumptions about how the world works and the best way to behave influenced my thoughts and actions, even though I was not always aware of this. For example, when a friend cancelled a catch-up, I would immediately assume they didn't like me. My lack of early experience in life with testing out my boundaries, processing my emotions, exploring my interests, and articulating my needs didn't allow me an opportunity to learn. As an adult, I had no idea who I was or what I wanted in life. It was not until I was able to free myself from the cloak of conditioning that I could explore what lay within. I learnt how to give myself permission to feel my emotions. I learnt how to prioritise my health and wellbeing, and I proactively put supports in place that were suited to my individual needs. I have learnt my limits and am much better at accepting them. I have intentionally practised self-expression and am communicating what I want to actualise in life.

Exploring our inner world creates more genuine connections with ourselves and others. Individuation encompasses the integration of the mind (to embrace oneself in its entirety, rather than being at odds with oneself), the pursuit of self-discovery (a deeper sense of meaning and self-discovery), and the interconnectedness of human existence (e.g., more fulfilling relationships).
Jung stated:

> 'Individuation means becoming an 'in-dividual', and in so far as 'individuality' embraces our innermost, last, and incomparable uniqueness, it also implies becoming one's own self. We could therefore translate individuation as 'coming to selfhood' or 'self-realisation' (Carl Jung, The Collected Works of CG Jung, Vol 7).

Getting to know your personal roadblocks is a critical step towards achieving overall mental health and wellbeing, as depicted in the following vignette.

I have picked myself up from ruin so many times. I have experienced a pattern repeating. When I find something I am passionate about, I give it my absolute all. If I am not offered flexibility to accommodate as needed, I will eventually become burnt out. I have experienced mental breakdowns that were debilitating and scary. When I could no longer function, I became extremely isolated and in fear of pursuing my passions. With the help of my psychologist, we were able to create a safe path that allowed me to understand my nervous system and accommodate my individual needs. I now feel the flow of operating within my own space and time, which is joyously expressive.

One of the benefits of obtaining an understanding of ADHD (particularly an understanding of hyper empathy and rejection-sensitive dysphoria) is that people learn to check in and honour their needs.

In my 20s, I was adventurous and travelled the world. My hyper-empathy meant seeing the best in people and giving to my heart's content. When I look back at unhealthy relationships in which toxic people sought to exert control over me, I feel compassion for my inner child and want to protect her beauty and adventurous spirit.

The following vignette describes a journey towards self-investment.

I was known to be good at putting out spotfires and problem-solving at work. People come to me for answers. As an employee, I was not credited for the work of helping others, as the workplace only measured pre-determined output. When I got home from work, I had nothing left for myself. I became reclusive. That led me to feel like a failure. With an understanding of ADHD, I have learnt to ruthlessly defend my time. I am time-blocking self-investment.

The following vignette moves away from an unrealistic and perfectionist pursuit for balance.

I cannot be expected to always achieve balance. Rather, a more realistic goal is learning strategies that allow me to identify what I need when I am dysregulated. I am accepting accommodations (e.g. time blocking to avoid over-scheduling), energy accounting (e.g., engaging in activities that involve being vs. doing) and seeking support (e.g., learning emotional regulation strategies).

My own personal journey with shadow work has been transformative. In childhood, I often felt that I was too much (e.g., too passionate, too sensitive, etc.). I irritated adults when I would question why things occurred. My inner child wished for a healthy adult to help me understand social norms. I attempted to repress my emotions, curiosity, and self-expression. It felt like I was limiting myself to a small box that dulled me down. I had been taught to push through and ignore what my body was telling me. This type of repression took its toll. I could not regulate, relate, or reason in a way that I needed to. The social fatigue of my persona weighed heavily on me. I was operating in survival mode, which exacerbated my anxiety (e.g., my thoughts were intrusive) and precipitated ritualistic behaviours (e.g., I would watch the same movie daily on repeat) and restrictive behaviours (e.g., I could only eat a restricted selection of food types). I engaged in unhealthy ways of coping (e.g., skin picking). Despite achieving academically, my mental health concerns and inability to function resulted in my need to drop out of school after year ten.

When I realised that I was autistic, it felt like someone had handed me the key to acceptance and understanding. A pathway towards wholeness involved unmasking from the social persona and embracing the shadow self, to no longer feel hidden and disconnected. I understood what safety (feeling regulated) and connection (feeling related) looked like for me personally. I was able to notice signs of dysregulation in my body and learnt coping strategies. For example, certain sensory experiences (e.g., a room full of people talking can be exhausting for me as I process the complexity of every single noise) and external stimuli (e.g., sensitivity to subtle external changes in an environment) impact me. I learnt to adopt a lifestyle that actively supports the regulation of my nervous system. Autism was so much more than a diagnosis to me. Self-realisation felt liberating. Integrating the parts of myself that were discouraged allowed me to focus my efforts on thriving as my autistic self.

Exploring my shadow led to greater authenticity, internal strength and conservation of my energy. I no longer diminish the intensity of my emotions, passions, or deep thinking. Self-expression feels freeing. I have embraced my sensitivity. I am naturally a curious person who questions things. I am a great advocate for being respectful of people's needs, including my own. I am ambitious and passionate. When I am in tune with my mind, it feels like I am moving through a boulevard of green lights. Although some people will try to demand that you fit into their box, that says more about their limits than mine. I feel a sense of autistic pride.

Chapter 16

'Your Brain is Incredible'

The noted US psychiatrist, Dr Edward Hallowell, specialises in ADHD and delivers a diagnosis to a child in a way that emphasises strengths and builds a healthy sense of self. Hallowell advises a twelve-year-old child, 'I have great news for you. We've learned a lot about you, Jeremy, and guess what? You have an amazing brain. Your brain is incredible. Hallowell uses the analogy of a Ferrari engine outfitted with bicycle brakes. Hallowell states, 'Your brakes are not strong enough to control the powerful brain you've got. So, sometimes, you race past places where you mean to stop, or you ignore instructions you mean to hear. But don't worry. I am a brake specialist. I will help you strengthen your brakes so you can become the champion you are.' Hallowell argues that leveraging a child's strengths leads to overall success and wellbeing as the child believes they will excel despite disappointment and defeat. Furthermore, this approach encourages a growth mindset that promotes resilience.

A strength-based perspective does not deny that disorders such as attention deficit hyperactivity disorder carry potentially life-threatening risks and disabilities. However, it also seeks to acknowledge the talents, interests, and skills upon which the person can build a life of success and joy. If a person is genuinely proud of who they are, it helps them to navigate the world better. In this way, expectations become more realistic and do not require the person to meet unreasonable standards.

One of the most challenging things I find about navigating the world with ADHD is when people don't believe that ADHD exists. I have enough struggles to manage in my daily life without having to justify my diagnosis. I have difficulty concentrating, focusing and remembering things. My symptoms of hyperactivity are not visible to others as I experience them internally. I experience hyperactivity as a feeling of emotional overwhelm and racing thoughts. Emotional instability is experienced as increased intensity of moods that can shift quickly. I have passionate thoughts and emotions that are more intense than those of the average person. I have difficulty letting go of thoughts, and I experience anxiety, periods of low mood and sleep concerns (e.g., difficulty falling asleep). I experience shame ('feeling undeserving') and rejection when I feel that I have fallen short of my expectations of myself. I am hypersensitive to sensory experiences. It is uncomfortable for me to work amongst background noise, such as in open-plan work environments. I use tools such as headphones to control or limit sensory input or remove myself when I can. When there is no option to accommodate my individual needs, and I have exhausted all my strategies for responding, I experience ADHD burnout. I should not have to get to a point of crisis before my struggles are believed.

Tailoring support to my neurobiological needs allows my body to feel well-resourced, and I can embrace the strengths and beauty of my mind. I have many strengths, including being passionate, honest, compassionate, good in a crisis (compartmentalise), intuitive, and creative. I am generally described as warm-hearted, and I develop genuine and meaningful friendships. I have a strong sense of fairness and justice. I am loyal, honest, witty, caring and articulate, with an active and curious mind. My acute sensitivity to sensory experiences gives me a remarkable view of the world.

Many celebrated innovators of past and present are known or thought to have had ADHD. ADHDers tend to thrive in situations of rapid change and variety, as well as environments that reward creativity and out-of-the-box thinking. The energy, charm, and euphoria of a problem-solving mind can create a wide variety of businesses that can positively impact society. Innovations that may improve our standard of living and can also create jobs and conditions for a prosperous society. Unfortunately, these perceived advantages may result in disruptive lifestyle choices, poor impulse control, increased substance abuse, etc. Increased optimism and grandiosity can lead people to underestimate/dismiss the potential negative consequences of their behaviour, rush into an activity or make decisions without carefully considering the pros and cons, and/or only focus on information confirming their beliefs whilst ignoring evidence. Individualised medical treatment is often necessary to achieve an overall sense of balance and prevent symptoms from exacerbating.

While supporting ADHDers to achieve self-care and balance is important, it is also important for them to follow their heart and trust that they will do things okay. A fear of fostering strengths, talents, and interests can leave people feeling disconnected and unable to value themselves. Embracing an authentic self is an effective formula for success. The neurodiverse problem-solving mind is not afraid to make mistakes or give things a go, and often, creativity is stifled by other people imposing their limits upon others. Problem-solving minds have a wealth of new ideas. Building a healthy self-concept can promote an eagerness to learn and the likelihood of developing a self-compassionate mindset that acknowledges that support is vital and needed. Neurodivergent clients have an admirable level of psychological grit, and they have worked incredibly hard to pursue answers.

References

Barkley, R.A. (1998). *Attention-deficit hyperactivity disorder. A handbook for diagnosis and treatment* (2nd ed). The Guilford Press.

Brown, Thomas E. (2005). Attention Deficit Disorder: *The unfocused mind in children and Adults.* Yale University Press.

Bubl et al. (2015). Elevated background noise in adult attention deficit hyperactivity. *PLos One, 10*(2), https://doi.org/10.1371/journal.pone.0118271.

Dana, D. (2018). *The Polyvagal Theory in Therapy: Engaging the Rhythm of Regulation.* W. W. Norton & Company, Inc.

Dana, D. (2020). *Polyvagal Exercises for Safety and Connection: 50 client centered practices.* New York: WW Norton & Company.

Dana, D. (2023). *Polyvagal Flip Chart: Understanding the science of Safety.* New York: W.W. Norton & Company, Inc.

Delahooke, M. (2019). *Beyond Behaviours.* Wisconsin: PESI Publishing.

Dodson, W. (2021). Recognizing and Managing Rejection Sensitive Dysphoria. *Attitude Magazine.* Retrieved from http://www.additudemag.com/rejection-sensitive-dysphoria-adhd-diagnosis-treatment/

Dodson, W. (2023). *ADHD Brain: Unravelling Secrets of Your ADD Nervous System.* Retrieved from http://www.additudemag.com/secrets-of-the-adhd-brain/

Jung, CG. (1972). The collected works of CG Jung, Vol. 7: *Two Essays on Analytical Psychology.*

Koelsch, S. (2014). Brain correlates of music evoked emotions. *Nature Reviews of Neuroscience, 15* (3), 170–180.

Leary, M., Tate, E., Adams, C., Allen, A., & Hancock, J. (2007). Self-compassion and reactions to unpleasant self-relevant events: The Implications of treating oneself kindly. *Journal of Personality and Social Psychology, 92*(5), 887–904.

Mayer, J., & Salovey, P. (1997). What Is Emotional Intelligence? In Peter Salovey and David Sluyter (Ed.). *Emotional Development and Emotional Intelligence.* New York: Basic Books.

Neff, K. (2003a). Self-Compassion: An alternative conceptualization of a healthy attitude toward oneself. *Journal of Self and Identity, 2*, 85–101.

Neff, K. (2003b). The development and validation of a scale to measure self-compassion. *Journal of Self and Identity, 2*, 223–250.

Neff, K. D. (2005). Self-compassion: Moving beyond the pitfalls of a separate self-concept. In J. Bauer & HA Wayment (Eds.) *Transcending Self-Interest Psychological Explorations of the Quiet Ego.* Washington DC: APA Books.

Neff, K. D., Hseih, Y., & Dejitthirat, K. (2005). Self-compassion, achievement goals, and coping with academic failure. *Journal of Self and Identity, 4*, 263–287.

Neff, K., Kirkpatrick, K.L., & Rude, S.S. (2007a). Self-compassion and adaptive psychological functioning. *Journal of Research in Personality, 41*,139–154.

Neff, K., Kirkpatrick, K.L., & Rude S.S. (2007b). An examination of self-compassion in relation to positive psychological functioning and personality traits. *Journal of Research in Personality, 41*, 908–916.

Oscarsson M, Nelson M, Rozental A, Ginsberg Y, Carlbring P, Jönsson F. (2022). Stress and work-related mental illness among working adults with ADHD: A qualitative study. *BMC Psychiatry, 22* (1), 751.

Perry, B. D. (2020). The Neuro sequential Model: A developmentally sensitive, neuroscience-informed approach to clinical problem solving. *Neurosequential Network*. Retrieved from https://www.neurosequential.com/

Perry, M.D. & Winfrey, O. (2021). *What happened to you: Conversations on trauma, resilience, and healing*. New York: Flatiron Books.

Petersson, M. et al. (2017). Oxytocin and cortisol levels in dog owners and their dogs are associated with behavioral patterns: an exploratory study. *Front. Psychol.*, 8: 1796.

Plessen, K.J., Bansal, R., Zhu, H., Whiteman, R., Amat, J., Quackenbush, G. A., Martin, L., Durkin, K., Blair, C., Royal, J., Hugdahl, K., & Peterson, B.S., (2006). Hippocampus and amygdala morphology in attention-deficit/ hyperactivity disorder. Archives of general psychiatry, *63,* (7), 795–807.

Porges, S. (2004). Neuroception: A Subconscious system for detecting threats and safety. *Zero to Three, 24* (5), 19–24.

Porges, S. W. (2009). The polyvagal Theory: New Insights into adaptive reactions of the autonomic nervous system. *Cleveland Clinic Journal of Medicine, 76* (4), 86–89.

Porges, S. W., & Dana, D. (2018). *Clinical Applications of the Polyvagal Theory: The Emergence of Polyvagal informed Therapies*. W. W. Norton & Company Ltd.

Porges, S. (2011). *The Polyvagal Theory: Neurophysiological Foundations of Emotions, Attachment, Communication, Self-Regulation*. W.W. Norton & Company: New York.

Porges, S. (2009). Reciprocal influences between body and brain in the perception and expression of affect: A polyvagal perspective. In D. Fosha, D.J. Siegel, & M.G. Solomon (eds.), *The power of emotion: Affective neuroscience, development, clinical practice*. New York: Norton.

Raymaker et al. (2020). Having all of your internal resources exhausted beyond measure and being left with no clean-up crew. Defining Autistic Burnout. *Autism Adulthood, 2* (2), 132–143.

Sansone, R. A., &Sansone, L. A. (2013). Sunshine, serotonin, and skin: a partial explanation for seasonal patterns in psychopathology. *Innovations in Clinical Neuroscience, 10* (7–8), 20.

Sprouse-Blum, A.S., Smith, G., Sugai, D., & Parsa, F.D. (2010). Understanding endorphins and their importance in pain management. *Hawaii Medical Journal, 69* (3), 70.

Tian L, Jiang T, Liang M, Zang Y, He Y, Sui M, Wang Y (2008). Enhanced resting-state brain activities in ADHD patients: A fMRI study. *Brain Development, 30*: 342–348.

Uvnas-Moberg, K., Handlin, L., & Petersson, M. (2014). Self-soothing behaviors with particular reference to oxytocin release induced by non-noxious sensory stimulation. *Frontiers in Psychology, 5*: 1529.

Volkow, N.D., Wang, G.J., Kollins, S.H., Wigal, T.L., Newcorn, J. H., Telang, F., Fowler, J.S., Zhu, W., Logan, J., Ma, Y., Pradhan, K., Wong, C., & Swanson, J.M. (2009). Evaluating dopamine reward pathway in ADHD: Clinical implications. *JAMA, 302* (10), 1084–1091.

Volkow, N. D., Wang, G-J., Newcorn, J. H., Kollins, S. H., Wigal, T. L., Telang, F., Fowler, J. S., Goldstein, R. Z., Klein, N., Logan, J., Wong, C., & Swanson, J. M. (2010). Motivation deficit in ADHD is associated with dysfunction of the dopamine reward pathway. *Molecular Psychiatry, 16* (11), 1147–1154.

Wu J, Xiao H, Sun H, Zou L, & Zhu LQ. (2012). Role of dopamine receptors in ADHD: A systematic meta-analysis. *Molecular Neurobiology, 45* (3), 605–620.

Yim J. (2016). Therapeutic Benefits of Laughter in Mental Health: A Theoretical Review. *The Tohoku Journal of Experimental Medicine, 239*(3), 243–249.

Young, J. E., Klosko, J.S., Weishaar, M.E., (2003). *Schema Therapy: A practitioner's guide.* New York: Guildford Press.

www.ingramcontent.com/pod-product-compliance
Lightning Source LLC
Chambersburg PA
CBHW040136270326
41927CB00019B/3403